COMMON SOFTWARE DEVELOPMENT MISTAKES MADE BY MANAGERS AND DEVELOPERS

Ways to eliminate poor quality software, business disruption and high technical support cost

By Ambrose O Akpotaire

Akpotaire, pronounced Ak po tai re'

COMMON SOFTWARE DEVELOPMENT MISTAKES
MADE BY MANAGERS AND DEVELOPERS
By Ambrose O Akpotaire

ISBN   1448652073
EAN-13   9781448652075

Trademarks

Microsoft Access is a registered trademark or trademark of Microsoft Corporation.
Microsoft is a registered trademark of Microsoft Corp.
Windows is a registered trademark of Microsoft Corp.
Oracle is a registered trademark of Oracle Corporation.
UNIX is a registered trademark of UNIX System Laboratories, Inc
Btrieve is a registered trademark of Pervasive Software.
JAVA is a registered trademark of Sun Microsystems, Inc.
Other products and company names mentioned herein are trademarks of their respective owners.

The book gives practical solutions to everyday software development missteps. However, the author, publisher, resellers and distributors do not provide any express, statutory or implied warranties and assumes no responsibility for errors or omissions, or for damages resulting from the use of the information contained herein.

Acknowledgements

The author thanks the following people for aiding in the proof reading of the book:

Helen Lee
Henry Gonzalez
Monday Anigboro
Pat Dames
Patrick Mosi
Ram Prasad
Raponia Hodges-Graves
Sam Young
Vanessa Morris

Dedication

I dedicate this book to my wife, Pam Akpotaire, for doing both mom and dad duties while I worked on the book.

I also dedicate the book to Joanne Price, RIP, and Henry Gonzalez for the opportunities they gave me to produce software that stood the test of time.

Contents at a glance

Table of Contents

INTRODUCTION

The goal of this book is to have software development teams produce high quality software by pointing out common errors and ways to overcome such errors.

The introduction contains some background information of the players in the software development process. It also shows how poor quality has become prevalent.

INTRODUCTION

Information technology has evolved rapidly both in quantity and variety. Just about every business has some level of automation or software tool. Large corporations have very complex network of systems and tools that must work together to accomplish business goals of the corporation. These systems may be scattered throughout several geographical locations including multiple countries, but tied together with a good network infrastructure. Most homes have personal computers connected to the internet to retrieve information or purchase goods and services.

With the growth of information technology, came very high demand for knowledgeable personnel to create software needed to make corporations and individuals function as efficiently as possible. Over time, software has become more and more complex requiring a team of many specialized persons to create any piece of software: requirement analyst, software designer, software architect, developer, project manager, tester, and many others.

The high demand for new software has resulted in considerable drop in the quality of software. The proliferation of poor quality software has resulted in another group of personnel, called technical support staff. Most technical support is done over the phone in specialized environments called "call centers". Some call centers have over a thousand persons. In order to reduce call center cost, several corporations in the developed countries now offshore this function to low wage countries.

Call centers answer calls from users who are having problems using particular software. The problems reported to call centers include the software not working at all, not able to handle particular operations, gives messages that users cannot understand, has input labels with acronyms that users cannot understand, is too slow, and many others. A call to any call center usually involves one or more unhappy persons: the caller, usually the customer and the support staff. From the corporation's point of view, the call center is a necessary evil required to please angry customers.

What will happen if a piece of software was developed so well that it worked all the time, handled all operations, gave meaningful messages that users understood, had intuitive screens that users understood, was fast, and had no other problems? I know what you are thinking; that's impossible. Anyway, there will be no more need for a call center, but more importantly, no more unhappy customers. For the sake of the unhappy customers, it should be a high priority of any software group to write software so well as to make call centers almost unnecessary.

By following the practices outlined in this book, which involves users, testers, managers and information technology staff at all levels, organizations should be able to substantially reduce the prevalence of poor quality software or eliminate it altogether.

As stated earlier, it takes a team to develop most software today and nearly all persons involved should share the blame when the quality is poor, resulting in a huge call center and lots of business disruption. This book highlights each team member's role and how they contribute to the quality of software. More importantly, it provides solutions on how to always produce high quality software.

The book is not about any particular programming language or technology/platform. Any mention of any particular software is for illustration only. It will not mean endorsement or disapproval of such technology/platform as the case might be.

WHO SHOULD READ THIS BOOK?

Anyone involved during the development/ maintenance of software should read this book and all non technical software users should read the first few chapters.

WHO SHOULD READ THIS BOOK?

Information Technology Managers At All Levels

Managers should read this book to understand how their emphasis on haste contributes to software quality and what they can change to improve software quality.

User Group Managers

The pressures to have software delivered in unrealistic time frames sometimes come from users and their managers within enterprises. This group of managers should read the book and learn how to demand high quality software from the information technology department without unnecessary pressure.

Users

Software users should read this book to learn the development process, thereby contributing during the development phase of the software. They should suggest meaningful business messages and intuitive screens to the developers, not technological messages as commonly produced by developers.

Software and Database Developers/Maintenance Staff

Developers with some experience will benefit the most from this book. They should be able to relate to the examples given. They should also be able to do better time estimate with quality taken into consideration and communicate such estimates to their managers.

Quality Assurance Testers

Testers should read this book to help design better test cases and ask developers better questions about the application. Like users, they should demand meaningful business messages and input labels to the developers.

Information Technology Students

University students in information technology should read this book for general information while in school and read it again once they have some experience.

Call Center Managers and Supervisors

Call center managers and supervisors should read this book, which will help them communicate ways to improve software to developers.

AUTHOR'S BACKGROUND

The author went from petroleum engineering to software engineering and brought his quality mindedness from petroleum to software engineering. He also learned some hard lessons early in his information technology career on what high quality software means.

Author's Background

Ambrose Akpotaire (pronounced Ak po tai re) has been in Information Technology for 23 years at the time of writing. He has held the role of developer, architect, designer, tester, supervisor, manager and many others. He graduated with a Bachelor of Science degree in natural gas engineering and prior to being a software engineer, was a petroleum engineer.

Before the personal computer was invented, most engineering calculations were done manually. Petroleum engineering, not being an exact science, required making lots of assumptions about rock formations. These assumptions have to be re-checked as drilling progressed and changes made to the drilling plan.

The petroleum engineering background has served Ambrose very well as a software engineer. Just as drilling plans need to be very flexible to accommodate rock data that are different from assumptions, software design needs to be very flexible to accommodate business changes, growth and invalid assumptions.

A drilling plan has to be checked many times by its author and reviewed and approved through several layers of management and operating partners because any mistake could cost lives and several million dollars. While most software errors will not cost lives, the triple check of the software design practiced by the author came from his petroleum engineering background.

Ambrose taught himself software development in order to automate a delivery service company, Dial N Dine, which he started with a partner. The company delivered prepared food from neighborhood restaurants to nearby homes and businesses. Software was needed to automate the delivery operation. The completed software allowed Dial N Dine to take food orders on the computer, send the ticket to the appropriate restaurant's printer and automatically send a message to a selected driver's alpha numeric pager. This was incredible because the internet had not been invented. This in-house developed software included accounting and other modules.

Ambrose learned quality software development the hard way. While working for a petrochemical company early in his career, he received what the company called "Epic Award" for quality from the president himself because users raved about its user friendliness and beautiful screens. Unfortunately, he was reprimanded two weeks later because his supervisor did not like the flow of his code. She complained it did not have indentations between "IFs" and "END IFs" properly lined up. While the code was correct in every other way, it was difficult to read. Another consultant was hired and Ambrose was amazed, watching him make the code look pretty (pleasing to look at) without changing any logic. He learned a lot from this tragedy, which has shaped his views of software quality. Very few developers have had the fortunate-misfortune, as they deserve, of being reprimanded for very poor quality coding.

Ambrose moved on to become a high quality conscientious developer in all respects and has created many applications that ran non-stop for years without a single support call.

The wealth of experiences gained from working with other developers (good and bad) lead him to write this book.

HOW TO USE THIS BOOK

Determine what sections to read.

HOW TO USE THIS BOOK

This book is written for a very wide audience, from chief information officers to students. The material is presented from broad, non-technical to more detail and technical. The early chapters should be read by managers and executives. These chapters describe the issues of software quality and some suggestions as to what managers can do to ensure that high quality software is being produced by their teams.

Subsequent chapters progressively get more technical. Quality assurance testers and call center managers should read from the beginning through the sections describing software labels and messages.

All development members, architect, designers, developers, and students, should read the entire book.

The above is just a guideline. It will be best for everyone to read the entire book. However, managers and executives might have both time and technical constraints, hence the recommendations.

TECHNICAL SUPPORT DEFINITION

It is necessary to define technical support as used in this book since the main goal of the book is to reduce technical support cost.

TECHNICAL SUPPORT DEFINITION

In the book, technical support covers two types of functionalities:

Technology staff whose role is to maintain software that is in production is considered as technical support staff. In some instances, especially in-house developed software, this is the only type of support available. They are the ones called by users when there is a problem with the software. These persons generally have high technical skills and are able to debug applications, correct erroneous sections of applications and enhance applications to accommodate business rule changes.

In other instances, technical support is provided by persons trained to help users with understanding how to use software. These persons are called when users are confused or the software is not behaving as expected. These persons do not generally have the skills to debug or change the software. They are able to help with setup and sometimes installation. This type of support is done from call centers when the software has a high user base. Problems that require maintenance are referred to the first group.

The reader should know which technical support is being discussed based on the context.

WHAT IS HIGH QUALITY SOFTWARE?

The title of the book may suggest that the book will start with a list of common mistakes followed by solutions. Instead, it is written like planning a journey. You first determine your destination, followed by how to get there. Then find out the obstacles you might encounter along the way and how to overcome them. This chapter is the first step to determining our destination.

WHAT IS HIGH QUALITY SOFTWARE?

Our destination is high quality software, but what is it? This should be a very simple question to answer. Unfortunately, the answer depends on who you ask. Remember the story of receiving an EPIC award and getting reprimanded for the same software (See about the author). In this example, the users found this software to be of high quality, while the information technology manager found it to be of low quality. They were both correct based on what they could see. If we asked the call center their view on this software, they would have said it was of high quality. On the other hand, the technical support staff, programmers who are responsible for bug fixes and enhancements, would have found the quality to be poor because the code was difficult to read, as the manager noted.

A simple definition of high quality software therefore is software that is deemed to be of high quality by users, technical support staff, information technology managers, and call center staff. If any of these groups consider software to be of low quality, the software is very likely of low quality.

In addition to the above, a more detail definition of high quality software should include the following considerations:

Requirements

High quality software must meet user's requests/requirements. Meaning it does, at a minimum what the users asked for. This definition of high quality appears to be the only focus of most developers and their managers. When software meets this requirement, users will most likely consider it to be of high quality. As we now know, this is not enough to consider software to be of high quality.

Environment

High quality software should run in its intended environment without interfering with other applications. This requirement is also quite easy to meet. However, I have seen poor quality software bring a million dollar UNIX machine to an inoperable condition by using up all its resources. When this happened, the machine that was designed to support thousands of concurrent users could not complete one task for one user. I have also seen a popular desktop application cause a personal computer to reboot every time a user printed a document. Software that meets users' requests/requirements but fail to coexist with others in its intended environment is not high quality software.

Failure

High quality software should never crash, unless the user pulled the plug from the electrical socket. Software that hangs, stops responding or simply exits unexpectedly is not high quality software, but we see this happen frequently.

Flexibility

High quality software should be flexible enough such that re-write/re-compile should be rare. The flexibility should allow it to handle all known business scenarios and handle new ones by simple configuration changes. Lots of software is written for a "perfect world" scenario such that any little deviation results in code modification. This is not high quality software because each code modification, even if it is one line, requires retesting of the entire software along with others with which it has to coexist.

Labels

High quality software should have meaningful labels. If it needs a user to enter social security number, the label should be "social security number", not SSN or SS#. This explicit labeling reduces learning curve and training cost of new users. It also reduces input of wrong information. The tendency to use SSN is based on the assumption that everybody knows that SSN means social security number. What happens if this same software is used in India or Africa? Most software (especially those designed for use within an enterprise) use too many acronyms.

Messages

High quality software should give meaningful messages when the unexpected happens. An error message of "File not found" is useless in most cases, but this is a very common message from a lot of software. A good message should include the particular file the program was expecting that it could not find.

Code Quality

High quality software should be of high quality code. This might sound confusing. A program might run flawlessly without frequent failure, suggesting high quality. However, if it is very difficult to understand by other developers when there is a problem, then the code is poor. There is a section devoted to high quality coding later in this book.

Summary

The above covers what makes high quality software but not in detail. The details and possible means to achieve these quality components will be in various sections of the book. Some of the details might be repeated in several areas because of the assumption that not all readers will read the entire book. We have enough information here to go to our next question; why is there poor quality software?

THE WRONG DESTINATION, WHY?

Our intended destination is high quality software, but often, we end up at the opposite end. Here is a partial list of the common mistakes and who makes them.

THE WRONG DESTINATION, WHY?

The days of one man developing a piece of software are rare. Today many specialists are involved: one specialist will create and maintain the database, another architect the application, another design the user interfaces, and others write the code. During or after development, yet another person will perform user acceptance testing. These specialists could be in one group or several groups as in larger organizations, where there are specialized groups such as the database group. Whether it is one group or several groups, they all have hierarchy of managers, leads, and etcetera.

The following discussion examines the role of managers of these groups that lead us to the wrong destination, poor quality. There is also mention of testers' and developers' roles.

Managers' Roles

Although the ultimate responsibility for producing good software rests on developers, managers and the culture of the enterprise play a large role.

Unrealistic Promises

Information technology managers sometimes make unrealistic promises to end users on how quickly they can deliver software before asking developers how long it will take to complete the development. This creates unrealistic time demands on developers. Developers start to work 16 hour days for months. Under such pressure, quality takes a back seat.

Organization's Culture

In large organizations, software teams compete informally, sometimes formally, for performance. Unfortunately, performance rarely means quality. Most often, it means speed to deployment. Managers in such an organization will always focus on speed, not quality. It will take training of managers at all levels to change such a culture.

Unnecessary Haste

Some managers simply like to brag on how quickly their team can complete a software development project even when there is no real external pressure. For some strange reasons, speed is generally valued higher than quality. Developers working under such management consistently produce poor quality software.

Expectation

Poor expectation becomes the norm when a team consistently produces poor quality software. Having manual processes or some other workaround in case of failure becomes sufficient justification to allow software to be deployed even when the quality is questionable. Somehow, the managers never demand better quality. The team gets used to fixing the problems in production where it cost more time to debug and fix code, not to mention business disruption. Remember that each fix means another trip to testing and deployment.

In the case of major vendor software organizations, they are comfortable releasing software with known bugs with the objective of releasing bug fixes. The clients of such vendors have come to expect poor quality and the bug fix releases that come after. Imagine if customers demanded some refund for each bug found in the software.

Reward System

Information technology managers often put their emphasis on speed of work, not quality. A developer that delivers software in record speed will be rewarded even if the software performs very poorly in production. On the other hand, a developer whose software never fails but takes longer to complete may be penalized. This happens because the rewarding takes place at the time of deployment (starting with all the praises for speed at the deployment party) or during the development phase.

The fast developer may have been promoted and moved on before everyone finds out that the software is problematic. In all my experiences, I have not seen any developer punished for software that failed often. In most cases, the developer was made to fix problems with the software if he has not been promoted or moved on to another development assignment. Even more unfortunate, the fast developer gets additional praises for fixing the problem quickly, instead of being reprimanded that the avoidable problem took place at all.

No Recognition

Quality minded developers get neither recognition nor reward. The only thing noticed about a quality conscientious developer is the time (mostly considered too long) it takes him or her to complete the software. Once the software goes into production and it never fails, both the developer and the great software is out of sight and out of mind.

Code Review

Most managers and software development team leads never check the quality of code produced by their staff. If the software has screens, viewing the screen is the most they will do. One reason for this might be the manager does not understand the coding language and environment. The manager may have written his last program 20 years ago in COBOL on a mainframe computer, while his staff is developing in JAVA to run on a Web server in a UNIX machine. If the manager cannot check because of limited knowledge of the language, he should have another team member or an outside expert do the checking.

For code review, see CONSULTING SERVICES at the end of the book or visit go2quality.com

High Turnover

High turnover rate among developers within development teams is one of the reasons poor quality software is produced. At the end of a major development effort, some groups will have an informal meeting to discuss lessons learned. Unfortunately, the group is quickly broken up to move to other projects with different players and managers. While the manager of the finished project may have learned that quality should have been more important than speed, the manager of a team to which the experienced developer is assigned, has not learned that. The developer who has just learned this cannot put lessons learned into practice, since the pursuit of quality will slow him down relative to his peers. The bottom line is the entire team has to raise quality to the highest priority, not just individual developers. This is why all managers' emphasis on quality throughout an enterprise is essential to the production of high quality software.

Quick and Dirty

Temporary solutions also known as "Quick and dirty" requests too often turn into permanent solutions. Sometimes, an emergency arises and a manager needs a very quick solution. A developer is asked to create a "quick and dirty" utility to solve the problem. This is a perfect condition understandably, if not a license, to write extremely poor quality software. The real problem is failure to go back and cleanup the code to meet quality standards. Managers should demand code cleanup of such emergency deployment. Not only do managers fail to demand the code cleanup, they may ask for more functionality be built on top of the "quick and dirty" solution because they are reacting to another version of the same crisis that led to the "Quick and Dirty" solution in the first place. Down the road, such software is deployed as a permanent solution, resulting in maintenance nightmare.

Training

Corporations are spending less on training because managers are not demanding training for their subordinates. There are now many developers that do not have training beyond college, in a technology world that changes at a blinding speed. As a result, such developers continues to code in outdated environments because that's all they know. Using the wrong or outdated technology could lead to poor quality software.

Quality Assurance Testers' Roles

Testing of software before it goes into production is a way to ensure the adequacy and functionality and sometimes, the quality. Very few quality assurance testers actually test the performance of the software to the extent needed in production. Testers usually follow scripts, based on the requirements. They usually do not demand that labels and error messages be made clear. When testers encounter unclear messages, they simply ask the developer for the meaning, log it and move on. They rarely ask for unclear messages to be changed. Testers should be trained and given authority to demand improvements beyond bug fixes. They also need to be trained to test far beyond the ordinary test cases which are usually based on perfect scenarios. If a program depends on a network drive, it should be tested without the network drive to see what messages the software will produce, instead of assuming the drive will always be there. I have seen software that simply hung and did nothing when the network was down.

Developers' Roles

Besides the above, there are several reasons why developers produce poor quality software. These will be discussed in more technical detail further in the book.

WHY SHOULD CORPORATIONS AND GOVERNMENTS BE CONCERNED?

The proliferation of poor quality software should concern every organization for reasons covered in this chapter. Unhappy internal or external clients will eventually lead to loss of prestige and trust.

WHY SHOULD CORPORATIONS AND GOVERNMENTS BE CONCERNED?

National Institute of Standards and Technology

US Study

The US Department of Commerce's, National Institute of Standards and Technology (NIST)'s study in 2002 reported: "software bugs, or errors, are so prevalent and so detrimental that they cost the U.S. economy an estimated $59.5 billion annually". With increased use of software and no additional attention being paid to quality since the study, it is safe to assume the cost of poor quality software has increased. Additional evidence for assuming decline of software quality is the frequent bug fix releases of vendor software these days.

This type of study is usually not enough to get organizations to change their culture. Somehow, managers may believe the study is talking about the government or other institutions, not theirs. What will it take for managers to care? I recommend each corporation embark on its own study. Determine the cost of avoidable software glitches. Take a one year old application and compute the technical support cost. Then add in the cost of reworking, testing and redeploying over a period of one year. Now compare this to an estimated increase in time that it would have taken to develop the software correctly in the first place. Most likely, the economics would favor high quality.

Sources of software

Vendors

Software vendors are companies that create a general purpose software tool or sophisticated suite of applications for vertical markets such as accounting packages. If it was possible to have a software vendor to pay its customers the cost associated with the poor quality of their software, some vendors would be out of business. It is only a matter of time before large corporations start demanding contracts with such payments. Even without such demands, many vendors have gone out of business because their customers lost faith in their ability to produce quality software. Software vendors should not wait for poor quality to make them extinct. They should change their culture and move quality to a higher priority while they still have customers.

In-House

The majority of software is developed in-house for internal use, as opposed to vendor packages. While it is unlikely that a corporation will go out of business for this type of software, the information technology department can lose prestige, when their users lose faith in them. IT managers must move quality to a higher priority because poor quality software makes it difficult for their organizations to provide quality service to their clients.

Outsourced

This is where a company contracts with an outside vendor to create custom software for them. In the past, companies resorted to this approach when they lost confidence in their own information technology department or they do not have available in-house resources. In the last few years, this practice has become common practice for reducing the cost of software by off-shoring the work. In this case, the vendor company is outside the United States or other developed countries. With off-shoring, there is more management overhead and greater exposure for data security and intellectual property risks.

Off-shoring

As stated above, this has become the preferred way to reduce the cost of software development by large corporations, based on the low wages of the country producing the software. Additionally, some corporations have also off-shored their technical support. Studies show that the actual cost savings of off-shoring is small and sometimes negative, when the additional resources needed to make off-shoring work are factored in. The information technology industry changes very fast and the persons that lead in innovations are those using the latest technology. In the past, the United States has been the leading nation. If off-shoring continues at its increasing pace, the United States will eventually have fewer persons with the latest technology. This is a cost that is unjustifiable by the small savings. In the long run, off-shoring will create a severe knowledge vacuum in the United States. Soon it will not be a choice to off-shore software development, but the only way even if off-shoring cost increases to uneconomical levels. Later, we will see that applying quality standards could save more money than off-shoring.

General Fallout And Cost Of Poor Quality Software

Support Cost

This has been mentioned in earlier sections but let's take a closer look by using a hypothetical situation.

Assumptions about a piece of software:

- Software has 60 internal daily users (20 per shift, three shifts daily), not unreasonable since some software have thousands of users.

- It was poorly written in 700 man-hours, about 4 months by one developer, because his manager demanded it must be deployed by a certain date.

- It has one dedicated technical support staff and an additional support staff for nights and weekends because the software failed 3 or more times a week.

- Each time it failed, it took an average of 30 minutes during the day and 1 hour at night to return to production.

- Developer cost is $100 per hour, which includes office space, benefits, etc.

- Dedicated support staff cost $80 per hour, which includes office space, benefits, etc.

- Night Support Staff cost the same as dedicated support staff.

- The users cost $10 per hour.

- The manager of the users cost $100 per hour, which includes office space, benefits, etc.

- The application was in production for 10 years.

Feel free to substitute numbers that you deem reasonable in place of the above assumptions and do the math.

Item	Cost of Low Quality	Cost of High Quality
The cost to develop the software is 700 hours X $100/hour. Estimated at $90,000 with code review for quality.	$70,000	$90,000
The cost of dedicated support staff is 2000 hour/year X 10 years X $80/ hour	$1,600,000	0
The cost of night and weekend support is 1 hour/week X 52 weeks/year X 10 years X $80/hour	$41,600	0
Users manager's time is ½ hours per incident X 3 hours/week X 52 weeks/year X 10 years X $100/hour	$78,000	0
Users downtime cost is 2 hours/week X 20 users/incident X 52 weeks/year X 10 years X $10/hour	$208,000	0
10 Year Total Cost of software	**$1,997,600 (about $2,000,000)**	**$90,000**

Many questions come to mind here: Why was such an application not re-written in ten years. The answer is the development team has moved on to other projects. The support team is not comfortable with major re-write and maybe re-write is a low priority on the support manager's list of daily fires. Let's assume however that the software was re-written after two years. The two year cost will be $466,000 plus the additional cost of the re-write.

Suppose this software was off-shored for a cost of $35,000 ($50.00/hour) and the quality was as describe above; remember that off-shoring requires more managerial overhead and the real cost will be closer to $60,000. The organization will save $10,000 off the $2,000,000 cost over the ten years.

Had this software been created using the methodology described in this book (see developer section), the cost may have been close to $90,000 with near zero failure over the ten years.

While the above is hypothetical, I have seen two applications of equal complexity run in the same environment by the same users for years; one had near zero support calls while the other had calls weekly.

Cancelled Projects

Another cost of poor quality software is in cancelled projects. The United Kingdom's Parliamentary Office of Science and Technology, reported in 2003 the cost of cancelled software was 1.5 billion pounds over a six year period. Once more, I believe each organization should conduct its own study to determine what cancelled software cost them.

The reasons for cancellation of projects are as follows:

Software did not meet basic requirements when delivered.

> This will usually be a relatively small percentage of failed software since quality assurance groups test business requirement functionalities.

Software cost overrun has become too high and project is still uncompleted.

> This is the reason for majority of cancelled software. The reason is the over-promising attitude of software managers. I have seen a manager cut a developer's time estimate in half because the manager believed the users cannot wait the length of time estimated by the developer. The manager did not question the rational for the developer's estimate, just that it was arbitrarily unacceptable. A possible solution to this situation is to add more developers to this project. The manager did not add more developers but still expected the project to be completed on time (the baseless time). In spite of the developer working 16 hour days, the software was not completed "on time", and the project was eventually cancelled.

One fallacy of managers is that the time to complete a project can be cut in half if you doubled the number of developers. You may reduce the time to complete a software development by adding more developers, but the reduction is never inversely proportional to the number of developers. The more developers, the more meeting times to make sure things work together and the more there might be wait periods because one developer needs a component being developed by another.

Business requirement changed mid stream.

This is less common but if the technology team had foresight and flexible design, many requirement changes could be handled by simple configuration changes. In the extreme, an inflexible design could result in project cancellation.

Human Resource Waste

In addition to the cost, having dedicated support staff is a waste of human resources. Some support staff should be spending time creating new software and meaningful enhancements, a bug fix should not be considered an enhancement. An enhancement should improve on high quality software by adding functionality and making the process faster and easier to use. This does not happen when the support staff is too busy putting out fires on a daily basis due to poor quality software.

Hidden Cost

Disruption to business every time software fails leads to frustration on the part of the users. The manager may be forced to explain to external client of the organization why their work was delivered late, leading to damage of the company's reputation. The user group will eventually have no faith in the information technology department.

HOW TO ENSURE HIGH QUALITY SOFTWARE

We have covered some common mistakes made by organizations which explain the high prevalence of poor quality. We have also justified that these mistakes are costly and organizations should be concerned. This chapter details ways organizations, managers, test teams and users can ensure that software meets high quality.

How To Ensure High Quality Software

The ultimate responsibility for producing high quality software rests with developers and the section of this book dealing with developers will teach them how. However, the overall organizational environment plays a very important role in the ability of the developers to produce high quality software. In an earlier section, we covered a partial list of how managers contribute to the poor quality of software. This section contains details of what managers/organizations should do to make developers produce high quality software.

Large Organizations/Governments

Individual departments of a large organizations or governmental entities may be able to change their practices and eventually start to produce high quality software, provided they are totally self contained and their managers are not compared to managers of other departments. Where the departments are not isolated from each other, the change in emphasis from speed to deployment to quality must come from the highest level of the organization. Performance evaluation from top to bottom should include software quality in measurable terms.

In the early days of industrialization, many workers lost body parts and many died due to work place accidents. Today, thanks in part to Occupational Safety and Health Administration (OSHA) of the United States, factories keep track of days without injuries. When injuries occur, they are reported and investigated in order to reduce their re-occurrence. As a result, factories and work places have become considerably safer and accidents that involve deaths make the evening news for days.

I do not propose a government body or regulation to help change our mind set about the quality of software. However, there is a parallel here. If each factory was left to decide if safety was important, the result would be different. Some will consider safety as slowing their processes and profit, failing to realize that injured workers cannot work which will equally slow down their factory operations.

Coming back to high quality software, each organization must see high quality as being profitable, as we have already shown, and demand it from the highest executive to the developers of software. Otherwise, some departments will continue to focus on speed to completion because that's how they are rewarded. As long as there is no enterprise wide insistence on quality and there is, at least, one group that emphasizes speed over quality, quality will eventually suffer everywhere.

Organization's Measurement of Quality

Each organization, large or small, should develop or acquire a central software quality reporting database. If the software was developed in house, the database should contain the names of the developers by modules, their supervisors and managers up the managerial chain to the top. The man-hours used to develop the software should be documented. If the software is a vendor package, it should contain the cost of the software, the vendor's name, contact person and means of contacting the vendor.

Each business unit or department should be required to report software failures to the database. Each report should narrow the source of the problem down to the module (which will identify the developer or vendor). The report should also include the following data:

- The severity of the problem (how long it took to resolve the problem).

- The number of man-hours spent from discovery through resolution, bug fixing, testing and deployment.

- The estimate of cost of the failure based on the man-hours and rates involved.

- Additional impact to operations and/or organization's clients should be estimated in monetary terms if possible.

- Indicate if this problem could have been foreseen and prevented by the development team.

- When business requirements change, enter the cost of modification (This will determine the flexibility of the software). If the software could not be modified, use the cost to replace it.

- **_Assign a number point of -20 to +20 to each incident._** This number system will be used to give the developer credit for flexibility and foresight (positive values) or debit for lack of flexibility and foresight (negative values).

The Point System, Negative or Positive

For example, a piece of software processes several files daily. It stops with an error message of "File not found". The support team looks everywhere and concludes that all files that the program usually processes were present and they become perplexed as to what file was missing. They ask operations to retry but the problem persists. It takes running the application in debug mode to determine that an initialization file used for making connection to a database had been deleted in error by someone. Identifying the root cause of the problem took three hours and resolving it took one minute. The developer should have known this error condition was possible. This incident should be assigned a negative value. On the other hand, if the error had been specific such as "Initialization file: C:\APPNAME\DatabaseConnection.properties not found", the support staff would have resolved the problem immediately. This shows the developer had foresight and should be assigned a positive value.

Here is another example: Suppose the same software gives an error message of "invalid file". The support team is able to determine the file being processed but cannot figure out what is wrong with it because the file contains over 50,000 records. Once more they go to debug mode and determines a day later that line 49,204 has a date value greater than current date, a violation based on a business rule. In this scenario, there will be potentially two pieces of software to enter into the database. The software that captures the data should have done the validation at input time. The software that processes the data should have given a better error message. Both pieces of software should be entered into the database with negative values. If error message is clear such as "file c:\inputFilename.txt is invalid because process date of line 49204 is greater than today's date", then the processing software should get a positive value. Again, resolving the problem would be minutes instead of a day.

For consistency, the actual values should be determined by a person or group, based on predefined guidelines.

The existence of this database alone will indicate to the entire organization that top management is interested in quality, not just speed to deployment.

This database will also allow organizations to get a handle on the cost of poor quality. If the software is a vendor package, the cost can be communicated to the vendor and if possible, compensation should be demanded.

Managers' Roles in Ensuring High Quality

Raises, Bonuses, Promotions And Awards

Assuming your organization has a software quality tracking database application, you must now incorporate quality into the performance evaluation of your subordinates. Raises, bonuses and promotions should take quality into account even if the developer has just been recently assigned to you. Do not reward developers immediately after the completion of a project. Wait three months of production evaluation before the reward.

There should be a company wide recognition program and awards given to teams, individuals and even vendors in recognition of very high quality software at one, two, five and ten year marks.

Standard

Have a minimum standard of quality and developers not meeting this minimum should receive training. Failure to improve should prompt an evaluation of their environment. Is the developer being given unrealistic deadlines? Under extreme cases, it might be necessary to take disciplinary actions against a consistent poor quality developer.

Time Estimation

The existence of the quality tracking database and the use of it will only frustrate developers and might even cause some to leave an organization if management does not change their ways. Managers must allow more time than usual for developers to carefully develop quality software. As we have already seen, the total cost of the software when support is factored in will be less on the long run. To achieve high quality, code review and other quality factors discussed in the developer section may take a little longer. With time and experience of quality conscientious developers, the additional time could become negligible.

Software Quality Training

The change to be quality conscious will not be automatic on the part of developers just because management gave more time. Most developers have acquired poor quality habit over several years. Developers should be trained on ways to develop high quality software. The few examples and pointers in this book are not enough. Achieving high quality will depend on the type of software. If software requires a database, the design of the database itself could cause lots of problems if the database is poorly designed. Therefore, the database designer needs training too. In a multi-tier environment, other considerations come into play, for which, all those involved need training, in order to develop high quality enterprise software.

New hires, consultants and even vendor employees, for outsourced work, should all take quality training classes. The training should be repeated periodically, every one to two years. Think of this training like defensive driving classes. Some drivers will drive with safety consciousness after a defensive driving class for about one year. Then old habits come back. It therefore makes a lot of sense to repeat quality training so that new school of thought in the field is learned and previous poor quality habits do not return.

For training, see CONSULTING SERVICES at the end of the book or visit go2quality.com

Technology Training

Less money is being spent on training employees these days. I assume this is part of cost cutting. For developers, this means they are limited in their exposure to new technologies. Naturally, they will solve problems with the technology they know. This leads to either insufficient or overkill software solutions. Managers should see to it that developers are trained on a continual basis so that they can use appropriate technologies for software developments. Elimination of poor quality software and the associated costs should be sufficient economic justification to train developers.

Planning

In large organizations, the process of software development involves a lot of specializations:
There is the requirements analyst who gathers the requirements; sometimes the developer will gather the requirement. Poor requirements gathering will automatically mean the software will have frequent change requests from the users. This by itself should not lead to poor quality software, but it will increase the cost of getting to the final stage of the software due to the numerous changes, testing and deployments.

Once all the requirements have been accumulated, the design phase will begin. The designer or architect converts the requirements to a form that will lend itself to programming logic. Then the choices of platforms are made.

There should be many reviews with the users to be sure all requirements have been accounted for before actual coding begins.

Managers should pay particular attention to the planning and design because this will make it possible to arrive at an adequate development time estimate.

Communicating With Users

A manager should be careful in communicating development time estimates to users. If you have experience with a developer who usually under estimates or tend to produce poor quality software, then you need to increase the time submitted by such a developer. The reverse is not true. It is not necessary to cut down the time of a developer who tends to overestimate unless the over estimation is excessive. Over estimate means the developer tends to complete his development before the time he or she estimated. This is good as long as the resulting software is of high quality. The user community will be impressed if a piece of software is delivered in six months when the estimate was seven months. On the other hand, the users will be disappointed had the estimate been five months. A five month estimate could also trigger a development cancellation.

Review

Checking the code is the single most important effort that will lead to high quality, but you must know what to check for. Looking at input screens is not enough. If the manager does not have the time or skill to check the code, he or she must assign the task to another developer or hire an outside consultant to review the code. The review process should be ongoing; not at the end of the development phase. It will be too late at that point. This approach should be used even for outsourced software. The things to check for are detailed in the developer section of this book.

Modification Reviews

All code modifications should be reviewed if possible. If a piece of software was initially reviewed and is of very good quality, a peer review should be conducted when changes are made.

Review Sensitivities

It is important to understand the sensitivities of code review. Each developer is proud (should be) of his or her work and a review by a peer may be uncomfortable to both the reviewer and the person whose code is being reviewed. The reviewer may thread lightly to avoid offending the peer. It is, therefore, recommended to have a group whose sole function is to review code. This group should be isolated from the developers. This makes the critique not personal and painful. Even more effective would be an outside consultant, for the reasons stated above.

Version/Revision History

Every source code should include the author's name, date and version. Whenever there is a modification, this section should grow to include the name of the person doing the modification, date, version and the reasons for the modifications. Software with screens may need a selectable menu to show the version history. This practice is another way to re-enforce quality consciousness. Most version control software can produce this information.

Outsourced/Vendor Packages

Just like automobile warranty, organizations should structure contracts so that contractors pay for technical support and bug fixes for the first three years of implementation. The cost charged by the contractor may increase, but it will be less than the long run cost of paying for bug fixes and technical support. Furthermore, this will be an incentive for the contractor to produce high quality software in the first place. Currently, the vendor makes more money if the software has bugs. The only thing they currently lose is credibility.

Quality Assurance Test Team's Role in ensuring Quality

The Usual

The quality assurance team is usually very good at testing the functionality of software by following the requirements document. Most developers are satisfied that their software passes quality assurance test. Unfortunately, the known functionality areas are not what plague most software. It is the environment. The software needs to retrieve a file from a network drive. The developer assumes the network will always be there. The quality assurance team will rarely ever test for possible network failure because that is very unlikely to be in the requirements document.

Beyond Requirements

The quality assurance team needs training on how to test beyond the requirements document. They should be trained to ask developers questions about software dependencies in order to create more in-depth test cases.

Regression

Regression testing should be done by test teams. This should be automated whenever possible. During the development phase, some groups deliver functionality in pieces to the test team. The test team may assume that the prior modules they tested is still good and only test the new functionalities. This assumption will not always be correct since new information may have caused the developer to change sections that had been tested.

Performance

Performance testing requires that the software completes tasks in reasonable time. The important thing to remember about testing for performance is that the test environment is as close to expected production environment as possible. If a production database table is expected to have 10 million records and the test is conducted with a table that has 100 records, production performance could be slower than test. Under such a scenario, the software could be unacceptable in production.

Exception

Exception testing is usually weak even when the requirements document indirectly indicates the need for one. The example given earlier of an "invalid file" error could have been prevented had a test team tested with invalid date and demanded a clearer error message.

Technical Support Team's Role In Ensuring Quality

Review With Other Teams

The support team is usually comprised of persons with much higher technical skills than the average user. Usually, the support team is trained on how to install and use the software. They are not usually aware of the most likely errors and dependencies of the software. They learn the problems as they go along, one incident at a time. This approach increases the length of time to resolve issues, which could give the impression of poor quality even when the software is of good quality. Prior to any software deployment, the support team should review the software with the development and quality assurance teams. In this review process, the support team needs to learn about all the findings of the quality assurance team, what error messages to expect and how to fix them. If error messages are not clear, they should be revised.

Standard of Quality

Maintenance support staff should understand the quality methodologies outlined in this book and keep all modifications to the same high standard.

User Group's Role In Ensuring Quality

The user group in most cases is comprised of persons that lack the technical skills of developers. However, they know what the software should be able to do. At a minimum, they should demand that input screens, labels and menus, be clear and logical. They should also demand a user manual, online help and input field hints. These should help to minimize support costs.

SOFTWARE DEVELOPERS, THE KEY TO HIGH QUALITY SOFTWARE

So far, we have not focused on developers. Instead, we have discussed the external forces under which the developer works. What will happen if all external conditions were perfect? Will developers produce quality software? The answer is no. This chapter details changes developers must make to ensure high quality.

SOFTWARE DEVELOPERS, THE KEY TO HIGH QUALITY SOFTWARE

Software Engineers

The term software developers and software engineers are used interchangeably.

Wikipedia as of March 2008 defined "Software Engineering" as follows:

Software engineering is the application of a systematic, disciplined, quantifiable approach to the development, operation, and maintenance of software. It encompasses techniques and procedures, often regulated by a software development process, with the purpose of improving the reliability and maintainability of software systems. The effort is necessitated by the potential complexity of those systems, which may contain millions of lines of code.

Let's examine the section of the definition that deals with quality.

"It encompasses techniques and procedures, often regulated by a software development process, with the purpose of improving the reliability and maintainability of software systems."

In particular, let's look at "with the purpose of improving the reliability and maintainability of software systems."

Reliability and maintainability is where a lot of developers fall short. Based on the current state of software quality, it is clear that many software developers do not fit the description of software engineer. In fact, no other engineering discipline will tolerate the quality of work produced by some so called

"Software Engineers". How long will a civil engineer keep his job if even one percent of the bridges he designed failed once within five years? "Software Engineers", not only keep their jobs, they get promotions and bonuses while the software they developed continues to fail daily.

The goal of the rest of the book is to get software developers to become software engineers by first understanding why software developers produce poor quality software and methods to improve the "reliability and maintainability" of their software.

WHY DEVELOPERS WRITE POOR QUALITY CODE

Please re-read the chapters "What Is High Quality Software?" and "The Wrong Destination, Why?"

In "The Wrong Destination, Why?" we discussed the role of the developers' work environment and managers, especially unrealistic deadlines. If all those environmental factors were remedied, what else would make a developer write poor code?

Inexperience

Due to the growth rate of the software industry, many developers do not have long years of experience. As a result, many write poor code.

No Criticism

Inexperience followed by lack of outside criticism cause developers to continue writing poor code even as they acquired more experience. This is the single most important reason developers write poor code. A good comparison is a dictatorship nation versus a democracy that has checks and balances. The democracy will tend to produce better results because the leaders are criticized for bad outcomes. A dictator is never criticized and, therefore, continues to make one bad decision after another, in other words, no code review.

Bad Habit

Developers have their tool boxes, usually pieces of code they used in the past. If the code was of poor quality and they did not know it, they continued to use it. As a result, bad coding is carried from project to project.

Quantity Over Quality

I have seen developers brag about the lines of code in their software. There are instances where a developer will write the same function several times in different areas of a piece of software. In other cases, it will be several slight variations of the same function. This type of approach will surely produce lots of unnecessary lines of code. The major support problem with this type of software comes when there is a logic issue in these functions. A developer fixing the code will fix some instances of the function and not others because he was not aware that others existed. Then the software is deployed and the issue surfaces again in a slightly different situation. All functions should exist only once per software.

Too Optimistic

Assumptions of environmental constants are usually too optimistic. As a result, developers fail to program for changes in the environment. A simple example will be the assumption that a network drive will always be present. Whenever the network drive is not present, the software will not give an appropriate feed back to the users, leading to difficulties in reaching a quick resolution.

Good Enough

I have actually encountered some developers, whom, when given suggestions on how to improve the quality of their code responded that the code was good enough. Good enough is not acceptable. It should be of high quality absolutely.

Procrastination

I have encountered other developers, whom, when given suggestions on how to improve the quality of their code responded that he was planning to go back and improve the code at the end. Unfortunately, he never got to the improvement part. This means quality should be the focus starting from the first line. It is easier at the beginning than later, if later happens at all.

Sample Codes

Books/internet sample codes usually promote bad examples. The examples are simplistic either because of their general purpose nature or the teaching process being conveyed necessitates simplicity. Unfortunately, lazy developers copy such code without renaming variables and functions to reflect their environment. In the end, such copied code is difficult to read in the context of the particular software. It will be like reading a book about New York and all of a sudden, there is a paragraph about Chicago. Just because Chicago is a large city does not mean it can be substituted for New York.

Requirements

Failure to consider all requirements is a problem. This means the software is not thought through thoroughly before coding starts. This leads to re-writes or insertions of code fragments in many areas. Some areas may be missed leading to bugs.

Wrong Technology

A developer will tend to use the technology that he or she knows to solve all problems even when it is not the most appropriate. A developer was asked to develop a program where the data resided on a Pervasive Btrieve database. However, he only knew Microsoft Access. His solution was to read entire tables from Btrieve into temporary Access tables, manipulate records of interest and save the tables back to BTrieve. This immediately made the Btrieve a non multi-user database since this application was replacing entire tables instead of records. The solution to this problem is more training.

I have seen a request to convert a browser based intranet application to client server because the users were disappointed with the performance. Sure, any developer that can develop a WEB application will have no difficulty with client/server (client/server would have been simpler to code and support). This goes to show that the most advanced solution may not be the right one.

New Technology Syndrome

This is when a developer focuses on using the latest technology to solve a problem when a simpler solution will do. In most of these cases, the developer himself is less experienced in the new technology which will lead to more errors. Furthermore, a higher level of technological professional will be needed to support/maintain the software.

Environment Utilization

In a client server solution, most backend databases have triggers, functions and other functionalities. Failure to fully understand both the backend and front-end technologies leads to over or under utilization of the environments. I have seen moving processes from the front-end to the backend improve a file load from 9 hours to 15 minutes. Again, the solution to this problem is more training.

Requirements Availability

There are instances where even the users are unable to properly define the requirements for software. An experienced developer could overcome some of this by creating a more flexible configuration and writing for more eventualities than necessary. Unfortunately, most developers will simply code for the limited requirement at hand, thereby causing lots of re-writes.

Consistent Labels

In a multi-tier/enterprise environment, proper naming and consistent messages makes communication between teams and processes easy to understand when there is a problem. For example, a file is generated from a workstation and sent to a mainframe computer for processing. The header record of the file contains the "Processing Date". On one occasion, the clock on the workstation was wrong by a month ahead. The mainframe reported the following error "DTF out of threshold" because the date is greater than today's date. This was a baffling error even to the mainframe support person. It took the mainframe support person reading the code to determine that "DTF" meant "Date of File". Even with knowing the meaning of "DTF", the message was still ambiguous. The file origination group used the term "Processing Date" while the receiving group used "DTF", meaning "Date of File".

Poor Design

The design has to be right. A bad design is equivalent to building a skyscraper on a foundation meant for a single story building. A skyscraper once collapsed because the owner added three additional floors beyond what the underlying structure could support. The design should fit the requirements, not the technology. Part of the design is choosing the right set of platforms. A stand alone application for one user with small volumes of data does not need a large database server. A developer with Oracle experience will quickly use Oracle for even a small application for one user. It will work but the support cost will be unnecessarily high. On the other hand, an Access developer might use Access where it could not handle the task, thereby causing lots of support issues too.

Jack Of All Trade

In small organizations, a developer may have to do analysis, design, project plan, architect, develop, test, code and deploy. Only more experienced persons could be good at all these tasks. As a result, developers in small organizations may develop poor quality software due to deficiencies in one or more areas of the development life cycle. Larger organizations will have multiple persons to perform these tasks and are less likely to have this problem.

WRITING HIGH QUALITY CODE

The previous chapter listed what I will refer to as general developer short comings. This chapter goes into details of producing high quality code, all of which is common sense. No new technology, but please read it because you may uncover one new "common sense".

WRITING HIGH QUALITY CODE

Please re-read the chapters "What Is High Quality Software?" and "The Wrong Destination, Why?"

If you are still reading, I assume you are either a developer or have been a developer in the past.

Since we are not talking about any particular programming language, I will use the word function to mean functions, methods, subroutines or any other names that mean this functionality.

Prior to this section, I have refrained from using words not commonly used by non developers. This will not be the case going forward although use of acronyms will continue to be avoided.

What Is High Quality Code?

The quality of software, as discussed in "What Is High Quality Software?" depends on who you ask: the users, the quality assurance team, and the support team. We will answer "What Is High Quality Code?" the same way but focus more on the maintenance support team. The support team will have reasons to actually read your code, in most cases, under considerably more pressure than you were in when you wrote the code. When the users of your software cannot continue because the software has crashed, they need quick turnaround so they can get back to work. The goal of high quality code is first to make technical support almost unnecessary. However, software runs in non-perfect environments, and on those very rare occasions when technical support is needed, your code should make the process as easy as possible.

High quality code is therefore one that leads to the least technical support cost possible. Below are the steps you should take to arrive at a high quality code"

Clear Logic

The code should be written in such a way that others can easily understand the logic. If you have programmed long enough, you must have come across code that took too much time to determine what was happening. Sometimes, this is caused by the developer using rarely used functions and constructs of the particular programming language. While the code works perfectly, it may take longer for a support person with lower level of experience to support the application. Use judgment as you code to avoid obscure parts of the language. For example, a C++ developer will easily understand that "Variable++" means to increase the value of "Variable" by one. A support person from another language may have a difficult time figuring this under pressure. Instead of "Variable++", "Variable = Variable + 1" will be very easy to read immediately. There is the argument that the first syntax is faster during execution of the code, but I do not believe the difference in execution time is worth the extra research time when there is a problem. Some developers write lengthy comment sections followed by difficult to understand logic. I do not discourage comments, but it should not be a substitute for clear logic.

Variable Names

Variables should be named such that what they hold is self evident. I am not talking about naming conventions such as starting the name with an "i" to indicate it is an integer. While such conventions are good, the name after the prefix should be meaningful. Variable "i" or "il" could be used to store line number of a file, but the best name should be "iFileLineNumber". With "iFileLineNumber", the reader does not get lost or have to go back and forth to find what "i" holds. I have seen developers complain that long variable names create unnecessary typing, which slows them down. This is the time to change your mind and look at the long term cost of the software.

Variable Re-use

Variable re-use is when the same variable is used for multiple meanings. The developers that re-use variables are usually the ones that have poor names. Suppose you need to read two files, OldFile and ModifiedFile, into memory for some comparison. You create a variable "i" and as you read each line of OldFile, you increase "i" by 1. After that you read ModifiedFile and reuse "i". Furthermore, you Start going through the array of lines in the files to compare them and you re-use "i" again. Depending on how well the program is written, what "i" holds at any given point could be confusing. A less confusing approach will be to have three variables, iOldFileLineNumber, iModifiedFileLineNumber and iFilesArrayCounter. Re-using variables can lead to bugs. What happens if you fail to re-initialize "i" to zero before the second file. You get the total number of lines of the two files, which may not have been your intention. Here again, a developer who re-uses variables is probably trying to save time. However, the time saved is nothing compared to the research time needed to understand what the code is doing when there is a failure.

Label Captions

Labels are objects used in most visual screens. They are used for giving textboxes meaning. Below is an example search screen. This will create unnecessary training difficulties as well as unnecessary support calls, especially with new users.

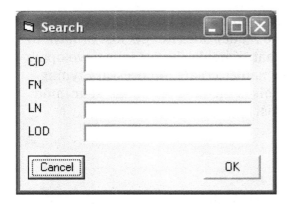

The above search screen contains four entries that are nearly impossible to guess unless you are trained or given a manual. In real world applications, there could be 30 or more entries with confusing labels. Now look at the same search screen modified below. Now no one will need a manual to use it, and there is less likelihood of wrong data entry.

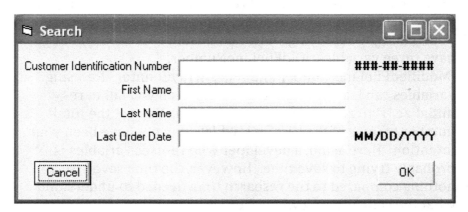

Screen Objects

Some objects are used for screens in applications. In the "Search" screen above there are six Label objects and four textbox objects. Many Integrated Development Environments (IDE's) provide default names as objects are placed on a screen during design. The names are usually as follows: label1, Label2 Label3, Label4, Label5, and Label6. The textboxes will have names: Textbox1, Textbox2, Textbox3, and Textbox4. I have seen very many applications where developers have retained these default names. In a real world application there will be many more screen objects with these default names. Leaving the default names will not cause the application to fail, but becomes very difficult to figure out when it fails for other reasons. Assume that there are six date fields on the screen and suppose we need to validate the "Last Order Date". With the default names, the logic will be something like this:

```
If Textbox4 > today then
     ShowError("date cannot be greater than
today")
End if
```

Please note this is not actual syntax for any particular language.

If this was a very large program, and a problem arose with a date field, the support person will need to open the form to find what Textbox4 contains. If on the other hand, the object had been named Last_Order_Date_Textbox, the code will look something like this:

```
If Last_Order_Date_Textbox > today then
ShowError("The last order date cannot be
greater than today")
End if
```

Now, the support person does not need to look everywhere to find the Textbox to which this logic is referring.

Objects like buttons will have code attached to them. These codes are executed when users click on the buttons. If you fail to name your buttons to reflect what they do, your button on click code will be called `Button1_Click()` or `Button2_Click()`, `Button1` and `Button2` being the default names given to the buttons at design.

A better name would be `Calculate_Square_Root_Click()`, if this button runs the calculation of square root of a given number. This will be clear to anyone that supports the application.

Database Objects

Most software today use database for storage. The design of databases is another book in itself. Just like screen objects, tables, columns and all other database objects should be given meaningful names to make problem solving easy and fast for support staff. Based on the screen objects discussion, it is obvious why table and column names should match their contents. Let's discuss something less obvious. In Oracle, as in many other large database systems, there is referential Integrity used for enforcing business rules. Let's say there are two tables, one for credit card types that contains "1, VISA", "2, Master Card", and the other, Customer Orders has a column called Customer_Credit_Card_Code. Customer_Credit_Card_Code can only contain 1 or 2. This rule can be enforced within the Oracle database with a referential integrity constraint object. If you create a referential integrity constraint object without supplying a name, Oracle will give it a default name such as "SYS_C002359". The numbers are generated internally by Oracle. If a user tries to save a record to the customer Orders table with a value of "3" in the Customer_Credit_Card_Code column, Oracle will produce the following error:

```
ORA-02291: integrity constraint (SYS_C002359)
violated - parent key not found
```

When a support person gets a call with this message, how long will it take them to solve the problem? The answer is much longer than necessary. Another answer is way too long. Why? There could be hundreds of integrity constraints in the database with these meaningless names. Suppose this particular constraint was named CreditCard_In_CustomerOrders_FK. Then the error message would be as follows:

```
ORA-02291: integrity constraint
(CreditCard_In_CustomerOrders_FK) violated -
parent key not found
```

Now, without calling the database administrator or digging through codes or documents, the support person can safely tell the user to enter a valid credit card code, at this time 1 or 2.

It is possible to catch this error message in the front end and generate an even clearer message to the user such as "You have entered an invalid credit card code. Please enter a valid credit card code before continuing". Even with this approach, a good database object name will make reading the frontend code easier.

You might be thinking, why not write two "if" statements in the front end application and give a meaningful message instead of the database integrity constraint? The answer lies in having foresight. What will happen if this company starts accepting American Express as a new method of payment, you add one record "3, American Express" to the credit Card types table and you are done. If the logic was in the program, this simple requirement will result in additional coding, compiling, testing and deployment. The difference will be one minute versus several days or weeks.

Functions

As stated earlier, the word function means all the various sub codes such as functions, methods, subroutines, etcetera. The name of a function should indicate what the function does. Some old programming languages limited the number of characters that can be used for naming variables and functions. To the best of your ability and within the limits of your programming language, name your functions so that anyone can guess what the functions do. Having a page of comments is a bad substitute for a non-intuitive function name. Most functions take parameters and some return values. The names of the input parameters as well as the return variables should follow the same principles as the naming of variables discussed already. In addition, the variable names should take their input nature into consideration.

To illustrate, take a look at the `filer` function below. It takes two parameters, an integer and a string and returns a string. Time yourself and try to guess what the function does.

```
String Function Filer(Integer No, String
digit)
```

Without reading the body of this function, there is no way to successfully guess what this function does. The word "`Filer`" may suggest it has something to do with files. Maybe it saves an Integer and a string into a file. To add to the confusion, the string parameter is named "`digit`".

Now, take a look at the complete function below. Time yourself and read through the function to determine what it does.

```
String Function Filer(Integer No, String
digit)
Integer i
String strCont
For i = 0 To No - 1
    strCont = strCont + digit

return strCont
End Function
```

Believe it or not; I got this function from software that has been deployed. Over 80% of the functions in this software were like the above.

The function basically had two lines of logic: A "for" loop that added the same character to a string. Then the string is returned. In other words, the function returned a string of a given length with all its characters initialized to a given character. Now that we know what it does, let's rewrite the function by changing the function and variable names only.

```
String getCharInitializedString(Integer
StringSize, Char FillCharacter)
     Integer characterPosition
     String InitializedString
     For characterPosition = 0 to StringSize
-1
InitializedString = InitializedString +
FillCharacter

     Return InitializedString
End Function
```

You can probably use this function now by the name only, without reading the body. If you have to read the body anyway, it should take less than half a minute to completely understand what it does.

Software Files

The files that make up your software should be named to make it intuitive to your support person. When there is a problem, the support person needs to get to the correct source of the problem as soon as possible. Suppose there are 40 source files that make up your software and they are called Module1, Module2 up to Module35, followed by Form1 to Form5. Now suppose there is a failure relating to the transfer of a file to another system. The support person will not know where to start. He or she will have to look through all the source code to find which one handled file transfer. If Module34 had been named FileTransfer.c or FileTransferModule.c, the support person would most likely look here first and most likely solved the problem faster.

Configuration Files

The same goes for configuration files. Use OracleConnection.properties instead of app.txt for a configuration file that contains connection strings for your database. Unless there is a need to make the content of the configuration difficult to guess, the variables inside should also have meaningful names. The following is bad:

P=1526
S=myServer.com

The above should be rewritten as follows:

DatabaseListenerPort=1526
DatabaseServerName=myserver.com

Why is all this important? By now, I hope you know the answer. If there comes a need to change to a different database, your support person can quickly find the configuration file and the values within to change. I have seen a 20 page long configuration file that was completely impossible to modify without first going to the program that used the values in order to determine what the variables were for. It is best to use several configuration files for your software, each one dealing with a specific task. For example, one for database connection, another for file transfers to another machine and so on. This makes it easier to find the place to change when necessary.

Log Files

Log files like everything else should be named in such a way that someone can quickly guess which application produced it. The content of log files will be discussed later under exceptions handling. For an application called CustomerDailyFileGenerator, the following are good names for log files: CustomerDailyFileGenerator.log, CustomerDailyFileGenerator _20080410.log. Once more, this will make it easier to resolve problems.

Input Validation

Data should be validated on input whenever possible. Too often, data is not validated on input where it can be corrected immediately. Either an output file generation or an input system downstream is made to validate and detect problems. Depending on how the downstream system is written, the problem with an input file can be difficult to determine. Suppose a downstream application is reading a file and finds a date value of 12/32/2007. Before we continue, I want to say this actually happened. Suppose further the file has 50,000 lines and the bad line is on 49,501. Solving the problem now will depend on the quality of the downstream application. Suppose the downstream application gave an error of "invalid input file". It will take days of looking at the file to figure out what could be wrong. If the application was a little better and it gave an error of "invalid date in file", then it might take hours to fine the invalid date. A high quality application should give an error message of "date value of 12/32/2007 on line 49501 is invalid". Now solving this problem will take minutes. In all my experience, I have not seen an application processing a file give an error message that pointed to the exact location of the problem. While downstream applications validated input files as required, their error messages are usually inadequate. Input file validation requirements are usually tested during quality assurance test, but usually with a file of 10 lines. It never occurs to the testers that in production, the files will be 50,000 lines and a better message will be needed to find problems. Worse than the 10 line file, I have not seen a test team intentionally put a bad date to see what will happen. The test files are always perfect.

The next issue with this situation is the correct value. What should the value have been instead of the wrong 12/32/2007? 12/30/2007, 12/31/2007 and 01/01/2008 are possible guesses. The source of the input could have been destroyed making it impossible to know the intended date value. This is why it is much better to validate data at input where it can be very quickly corrected and never cause unnecessary problems downstream.

I have seen developers say it is not necessary to validate input since a downstream application will validate the output file. To them, this is unnecessary double work that will only slow them down.

Logic Repeat

I have seen the same logic repeated in software such that if the logic is wrong, one has to look at several places to fix it. Otherwise, the same problem comes up again in a slightly different scenario. This usually perplexes the support person who feels they just fixed that problem.

Exception Handling

There are two types of errors that developers deal with. One is actually validation, meaning if a user types in alpha characters instead of numeric characters, the software should validate and give the user an intuitive message. The other type is supposed to be unexpected errors. I say supposed to be unexpected because most of the unexpected errors in software could be anticipated if developers did not make assumptions that are too optimistic. Being too optimistic, the developer of our "Filer" function did not include any error handling. Since the function has only two simple lines of logic, it appears nothing can go wrong. Here is the function again"

```
String Function Filer(Integer No, String
digit)
Integer i
String strCont
For i = 0 To No - 1
    strCont = strCont + digit

return strCont
End Function
```

What will happen if the input parameter "No" was assigned a number that was larger than the maximum string length for this environment? The compiler may give its own error "Maximum string length exceeded". Imagine a user calls a support person to report this error. Where will the support person look to solve the problem? It may never occur to the support person that the error is coming from this simple function. A support person will tend to look in the more complicated functions because he or she will make the same optimistic assumption that the simple function could not produce any errors.

Now let's add error handler to the code.

```
String Function Filer(Integer No, String
digit)
Integer i
String strCont
For i = 0 To No - 1
    strCont = strCont + digit

return strCont

ErrorSection:

ShowError ( err.message + " in function
Filer, source file Utilities.c")

End Function
```

This time the error message will be "Maximum string length exceeded in function Filer, source file Utilities.c". The problem will be much quicker to resolve now.

The best quality option will be to validate the parameters in addition to the error handler. Here is the function again with validations:

```
String Function Filer(Integer No, String
digit)
Integer i
String strCont
If No > length(String) then
ShowError ("Error in function Filer, source
file Utilities.c.  Input parameter 'No' value
of + No + exceeds the maximum string size of
" + length(String))

return ""

End if

If length(digit) <> 1 then
ShowError ("Error in function Filer, source
file Utilities.c.  Input parameter 'digit'
can only be one character)

return ""

End if


For i = 0 To No - 1
    strCont = strCont + digit

return strCont

ErrorSection:

ShowError ( err.message + " in function
Filer, source file Utilities.c")

End Function
```

Remember, we discussed the name of this function and the names of its variables earlier. Now that we have added error handlers and validations, please take a few minutes to re-write this function with appropriate names. As you will discover, the time to write this function to be of high quality is not significantly more than the very poor beginning, but the high quality version could save hours in support cost on the long run.

Performance

If your software worked all the time and never crashed but it always took too long to accomplish tasks, the software is still of low quality. An example was a program that loaded a file daily into oracle database. On a typical day, it took 9 hours to complete the load. On heavy volume days it took as long as 12 hours. If an error occurred during a load, it had to be restarted. Restarting created a backlog into the next day's file. The problem was remedied by optimizing Oracle insert statements through the use of PLSQL instead of regular SQL. After remediation, the load took 15 minutes on average. This is an extreme example but delays of one minute or more to save a screen to database can frustrate users.

The key to performance is to understand your environments and maximize the capabilities of each subsystem. In a client server architecture, the bottle neck, if any, will be the database (may be improper indexing), the network between the front-end and the database, and on rare occasions, the front-end software itself.

For those that have "object oriented" environments, be careful about too many objects handling the same data, it could be excessive, leading to poor performance. For reasons of being an object purist, some applications will have ten different objects, each slightly different but handling sub sections of a database record. When a record is fetched from the database, it is already in an object and the values can be retrieved and used by many functions of the application. Unless it is necessary, probably due to special processing or combination with several other data sources, you should not stuff the data into other objects before using it.

Feedback

If your application has screens, you should provide continuous feedback. Have a progress bar and show the task being performed. Lack of feedback creates the impression that the application is slow. Feedback will allow an experienced user to detect situations where the application has stopped working.

Logging

Log major events and all errors to a log file or database, whichever is appropriate for your environment. This makes support easier. Sometimes, users will report seeing one thing when something else is actually happening. The logs are much more reliable than the users report under these circumstances.

Platform

Choose the appropriate platform. Don't structure multi-tier when client-server is adequate. Some developers choose the technology that's most complex even for simple jobs. This is usually more for their self importance and job security than the requirements of the software. Even if all works well, a higher level of technical expertise than necessary will now be required to maintain the software.

Possible Options

Educate the users on what is technologically possible. During requirements gathering, educate the users as to what is possible, not just what they ask for. I have witnessed an application that made users enter the same data into several screens based on various purposes. In an application that schedule personal for shift work, the users had to type the names of each shift worker for every shift. The developer programmed it this way because the users told him this is what they did on paper. While the software worked, it is considered to be of poor quality since it did not save the users time compared to manual work. The developer could have educated the users that he could provide the list of all workers and have the user put a check mark next to workers for the shift they were creating, instead of typing the same names daily over and over.

Hard Coding

Avoid hard coding at all cost. Use configuration files or database for just about everything, even those processes that your user guarantees will never change. For example, suppose your application creates a file, transfers the file through file transfer protocol to another computer and deletes the original file. It might seem a great idea to create this process by pressing one button. If you could think ahead of the users, you will see there might be a need to view the file before or after it is sent. There might be a need someday to not create the file systematically but stage a manually modified file and send it. There might be need to send the file to a different machine or directory. The File transfer protocol ID and password could change. Every one of these possible scenario requires configuration options. The more configuration option you have, the longer the software could be in production without any rebuilds/recompiles.

Environment

Your software should fit into its environment without interfering with other applications or allowing other applications to interfere with it. The ability to accomplish this task has less to do with quality, but more to do with the technology chosen. On the windows operating system, several applications may depend on a single Dynamically Linked Library (DLL). If your application is one of these, then your application may fail if another application installs a version of the DLL different from yours. In the same way, other applications may fail if your application installs a different version from the one they were using. You must therefore know your intended environment and make sure your DLL versions are compatible with those in use by other software.

Obsolete Data

Delete obsolete generated files and database records. If your application generates files daily or creates database records, the application must include processes for deleting aged files or database records. No matter how large of a disk space you have, it will get filled up given enough time. I have seen too many support calls that resulted from disk being full. Most applications are not coded to detect full disk conditions. Therefore, they might report an error that takes hours to figure out when the root cause is the disk being full.

Documentation

All software should have both a systems and user document and these should be updated when the software is changed.

Code Review

Allow others to critique your code. This is very painful to developers but the organization needs it. Every developer is proud of his or her work and will feel stepped on if another developer or manager were to criticize their coding practice. Developers must change their mindset and see code review by others as an opportunity to improve themselves. One of the fears of code review is style. The truth is any given software can be coded in a 100 different ways. Therefore the person doing the criticism should be careful not to mistake a different style from theirs as bad coding.

After reading this book, peer code review should be a little easier. If code could just meet the suggestions listed so far, it will be very easy for others to maintain.

Others

It is not possible to list every pitfall and technique a developer should know in one book. Some technology environments have their own dos and don'ts. Two web servers may have different requirements on file placements and file extensions. Each development language has areas that a developer must fully understand to produce optimized code. Databases will have different strengths and weakness. All of these must be taken into consideration in addition to all the common sense approaches discussed here.

TECHNICAL SUPPORT

Technical support staff can play a role in reducing support cost both during the development process and production by providing good feed back to developers. More importantly, the support department can reduce support cost by properly training their staff.

TECHNICAL SUPPORT

Technical support is where the cost of poor quality software is felt and almost all software requires some technical support. The objective of this book is to offer organizations the means to reduce technical support cost to a minimum. This chapter will look at typical support calls and ways to minimize them.

Please re-read "Technical Support Definition" section again before continuing.

Below are typical support calls:

Password Expirations And Lockouts

Password expiration or user lockout due to entering wrong password more than three times is a very frequent support call. This is not due to poor quality software. However, there are measures organizations and developers can take to reduce these types of support calls:

Create a single sign-on system and have all software use its interface for authentication. While this will not eliminate this type of call, it will reduce it to one password system instead of 10 or more, each expiring at different times. With many systems, some users may use some applications so infrequently that they forget their password or by the time they use the software again, their password has expired.

Create Password management and alert system. In the absence of a single sign-on system, an alternative will be a password management and alert system. Not all software can interface with a single sign-on system. For these, each user should be given an account in a system that keeps track of applications, account numbers, passwords, password change interval, and date of last password change. The system will alert the users about applications where their passwords are about to expire. It will also tell users their passwords if they forgot. Under this scenario, the only account related technical support call will be related to the master password management system. Once more, this will not eliminate account related calls but will substantially reduce them. One major advantage of this system is that it will discourage users from writing their passwords on paper where they could be seen by others. The caution here is that the password management system must be a high security system where even the system's administrator cannot see user's data.

There are ways to enable workstation sign-on to integrate into applications' authentications. The technical detail of that is beyond our scope here.

Inexperienced Users

Ordinarily, there should be trainers among the user group to train new employees. Unfortunately, some user groups use technical support staff as trainers in informal ways. The new user uses the software improperly and calls for technical support. The obvious solution to reducing this type of support call is to ask the user group to properly train new employees, and to only call for support if there are true system problems.

I have witnessed the same software being run in almost identical manner by two user groups in two separate locations. One group called for technical support on average, ten times per week. The other group called for support on average once per week.

While the underlying cause was the poor quality of the software, the group with lower support calls had a more technically competent manager, and he took it upon himself to train his team on the software beyond the usual input screens. His team knew what happened beneath the screen and could solve many of the problems created by the software without calling for technical support.

Improper Usage And Poor Training

Just like the inexperienced user, experienced users also occasionally use software improperly. They might enter wrong data or run processes in the wrong sequences. This usually happens due to poor training or users hurrying to complete tasks. Running processes out of sequence can be controlled by well designed software, if there is code to check for the completion of prerequisite task before allowing users to proceed. As much as possible, validating input at the time of entry will reduce wrong information. More training of users will also reduce these types of support calls.

Caliber of Users

During the development phase, developers usually deal with the managers of the user group, not the users directly. In some cases, the direct users may not have been hired. The developer most likely will make optimistic assumptions as to the caliber of the users. Suppose one assumes that a user understands basic operating system commands and has the ability to navigate through the file system. This simple assumption will influence how an application is coded. In the end a user is hired that has no knowledge of computers beyond following simple instructions to perform specific data entry tasks. Now if the program was well written and it gave error of a particular file not being found, this user will still call for technical support. They will not be able to check the file system or try to determine why the file is not present. The solution is to assume that your users know very little about computers, and add possible correction instructions to error messages. The user groups should also make an effort to hire persons with enough computer skills to avoid excessive support calls.

High Turnover

A user group with a high turnover rate will create more support calls than normal. There is not much a developer can do about high turnover rate. However, following the recommendations of the prior three topics, Inexperienced Users, Improper usage and Poor training, and Caliber of Users, should help to minimize the support calls from a high turnover environment.

Acronyms

Excessive usage of acronyms can be very intimidating to new employees. Suppose there are 40 systems in an organization that are interdependent on each other and all their names are acronyms. You may have seen system diagrams with such acronyms everywhere. Let's just say two of them are called COES and SMTS. How easy will it be to remember these acronyms? Eventually, older employees start making verbs out of these acronyms. I have seen FTPing, from the acronym FTP. After the acronym names for the systems come acronyms for files and reports. If you are new to an organization, you will be completely lost in meetings because of excessive use of acronyms. With this type of environment, both new support staff and new users will have steep learning curves, followed by unnecessary difficult communications when there is a support issue. The solution is to reduce acronyms to a minimum, both in software screens and documents.

I bet you are eager to know what COES, FTP, and SMTS stand for. COES stands for Customer Order Entry System, FTP stands for File Transfer Protocol, and SMTS stands for Shipping Management and Tracking System. They don't seem so complicated once you know the actual names. The names actually tell you what these systems most likely do. The output files and reports, if named explicitly, will make it quite easy to communicate issues between users and support staff.

In an actual production environment, a new user was trained and told the software creates a file, encrypts the file and transmits the file to another system. The user called support one day stating that the encryption failed. This got the support technician researching for hours why the encryption may have failed. After he was completely exhausted, he called the user and asked how did you know the encryption failed? The user said the message on the screen stated "FTP failed". Not knowing what FTP stood for, the user assumed "FTP" was the encryption process. Had the message been "file transfer to mainframe failed", several hours of research could have been avoided. Upon knowing the true problem, the support staff quickly determined that the password on the receiving system had expired.

Confusion

Users sometimes call for support due to confusion. The input screen has too many acronyms or instruction steps are not clear. Calls due to confusion can be minimized by the development processes already discussed under "What Is High Quality Code?". You will think confusing scenarios would have been corrected in user acceptance testing. As stated earlier under "User Acceptance Testing", the focus of testers is strictly making sure that requirements have been met. Even if they point out potentially confusing situations, they do not insist on changes. They are satisfied with explanations, which mean users will continue to receive this explanation when the software is deployed. Developers should take it upon themselves to revise their screens or instructions to eliminate confusions even if testers do not demand it. If one person is confused, potentially, many more will be confused when the software is deployed, thereby generating unnecessary technical support calls.

Exception Handling

This generates lots of technical support calls. When a developer fails to handle errors, the complier gives its default error message, which is generally non-specific to the business and totally confusing to users. As discussed already, developers should handle errors in all functions and give meaningful messages. When messages are meaningful enough, the users might be able to resolve problems, thereby avoiding a support call.

Performance

Poor performance leads to lots of support calls. Most times, the call will state that the system has died or not responding. Some users may re-boot a machine, causing additional problems of corrupt or incomplete data. Developers should tune their software, taking advantage of each subsystem for maximum performance. Performance issues are frustrating to users even if the software completes all tasks eventually.

In severe situations, software can be abandoned and project cancelled. I saw a major development for a company that had manufacturing sites worldwide. The software needed to gathered information from all sites daily. Unfortunately, it took 26 hours on average to complete. The project was eventually abandoned until another consultant was hired to evaluate the software. With changes to the database and the topology of the application, the system completed its tasks in 1 hour. The original project cost $500,000 in 1987 and the revision cost $60,000. This was a success story, considering the relatively low cost to revise the software. The entire $500,000 project could have been thrown away.

Users can still call to complain of poor performance even in a well tuned application if the software does not adequately and continuously communicate to the user. See the two screens below and guess which will likely create unnecessary poor response support call.

Program generating file and showing hourglass

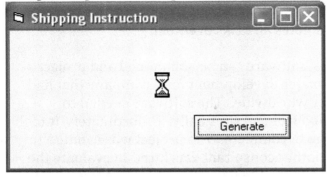

Program generating file and showing message and progress

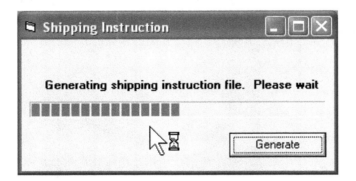

Assuming the code behind the two screens is the same, the first screen with the hourglass only will generate more support calls of the slow performance type. Assuming the process has several steps, the message and progress combination will give the user continuous feed back. Thus, the user will measure response by tasks instead of the full process. Please note that feed back is not a substitute for poor performance. It should be added to already great performing software.

Unstable Environment

There is not much a developer can do about unstable network or database or other hardware that have been provided to him. In all development however, developers should never take resources for granted. All file operations should pass through a common module to handle file related errors. Thus, an appropriate message can be given to users. All database operations should pass through a common module to handle dropped database connection related errors. The same goes for other hardware like scanners and removable drives. With proper error messages, the users may retry or call the network group instead of calling the software support team. Basically, support calls will be minimized with high quality software even in an unstable environment.

Inability To Restart Process

I have seen hours wasted because a process could not be restarted. This is one of those situations where the developers assumed zero failure. For example, a program loads information into a database from a file. There is no code in the program to handle duplication. If the program failed or there was power failure during the load, the users cannot simply restart the load because it will either create duplicate records or crash due to primary key violations. A support person must now go to the database to manually delete records. If the support person is not careful, he may delete records besides the duplicates and create additional problems. Developers must incorporate ability to restart all processes. This will avoid support calls of this nature.

Software Does Not Handle All Business Cases

This situation is caused by the software not meeting all business requirements. Either the developer failed to code the requirement or it was never communicated. If it was communicated, the quality assurance testers should have caught it. Sometimes, users try to make the software accomplish a task for which it was not designed. Today, most cell phones have Bluetooth, but Bluetooth has several profiles (capabilities). Not all cell phones implement all Bluetooth profiles. Therefore, a support person for a cell phone company may get a support call because the user's phone is unable to connect to the integrated Bluetooth in their car.

The solution to reducing this type of support call is thorough requirements gathering, testing and adequate communication of a software's capabilities to users.

Wrong Logic

Support due to wrong logic is a small fraction of total support calls. In this situation, the logic in the software is wrong and it produces the wrong result. The only solution is to fix the wrong logic. All the programming techniques already described should help to minimize logic errors and speedup the correction if errors are found.

CASE STUDY, SOFTWARE DEVELOPMENT PROCESS

We will go through the thought process and look at the typically overlooked considerations by developers. Once again, this will all be common sense.

CASE STUDY, SOFTWARE DEVELOPMENT PROCESS

For the rest of the book, we will go through the motions to develop a piece of high quality software. Unfortunately, we cannot create an application that we can compile and run, because we will not use a particular programming language. Just like all previous sections of the book, the goal is to point out common practices and ways to improve them, thereby achieving high quality.

For this software, we will create an imaginary company and its environment. We will then get requirements and proceed through the development life cycle. The process will be far less detailed than you would have in a real life situation, but applying the pieces should help you arrive at high quality software, no matter how complex your real life situation might be.

THE COMPANY

The name of our imaginary company is "NotReal Corporation". If by any coincidence, a company of the same name actually exists, we are not referring to such an existing corporation.

NotReal Corporation manufactures robots. The robots come in various sizes and each is programmed to handle specific tasks. Some are toys for children. There are several suppliers of parts and supplemental products for NotReal Corporation's robots. NotReal Corporation sells its robots and other third party products in its own stores, through its sales force, other retailers and through the internet. NotReal Corporation is a large organization with manufacturing sites in six countries and sales offices and other corporate offices in forty countries. It has 200,000 employees, 30,000 in software development. The company is only ten years old and growing rapidly.

As you can imagine, NotReal Corporation has a very large network, servers of all sizes and operating systems, databases, mainframes, hundreds of applications and tools, and thousands of workstations.

NotReal Corporation is a place where poor quality software can really do a lot of damage. If the robots failed frequently due to poor quality software, NotReal Corporation will be out of business very quickly. If the robots were perfect, but the business software, for example, its internet application is of poor quality, sales will suffer. Technical support staffs need very high quality software in order to help the corporation's clients.

Don't get discouraged, we are not about to develop the entire NotReal Corporation in this book. This background is meant to create the large picture so that we can have a better feel when evaluating our requirements.

THE SOFTWARE

Request For Software

All 1500 members of the sales staff have been issued a new sophisticated cell phone. The sales department is requesting that the information technology group create a piece of software on the cell phone that will allow sales staff to do the following:

Take orders from clients.

Create new clients and update client information.

Retrieve new and updated product information from the central database.

Upload the orders and new clients' information to the central database.

THE MOMENT IS HERE, SOFTWARE DEVELOPMENT

Requirements Gathering

What are the pieces of information we need to accomplish our goal?

We need the structure of the central database. Specifically, we need the tables that relate to clients setup, the products and orders tables.

We need the programming API and capabilities of the cell phone, especially its internal storage capacity.

We need a machine to host the server application which will respond to the cell phones and communicate with the database. We currently have 1500 potential users (the sales staff) of the new software. We should at least plan for a 3000 user community since we already know that NotReal Corporation is growing rapidly.

The Database

Suppose we place a request to the database administrator for the structure of the database as it relates to products, orders and clients, and the following pages of information are sent to us.

Report From Database Administrator

Table Name:	Prod		
Column Name	Data Type	Key	Required
ID	Number(10,0)	Primary	Yes
PN	String(100)	Index_1_1	Yes
Mod	String(100)	Index_1_2	Yes
Ver	String(10)	Index_1_3	Yes
Desc	String(1000)		Yes
Rel_Dt	Date		Yes
Ret_Dt	Date		
Cr	String(20)		
Sz	Number(5.0)		
Wght	Number(10.4)		
Wdth	Number(10.4)		
Lnth	Number(10.4)		
Heht	Number(10.4)		
Image	blob		
Manu	String(100)	Index_2_1	Yes
Prop_1	String(1000)		
..			
..			
..			
..			
..			
..			
..			
Prop_50	String(1000)		

There are 50 Prop columns numbered Prop_1 to Prop_50

Table Name:	SKUS		
Column Name	Data Type	Key	Required
SKU_No	Number(10,0)	Primary	Yes
KN	String(100)	Index_1_1	Yes
Mod	String(100)	Index_1_2	Yes
Ver	String(10)	Index_1_3	Yes
Desc	String(1000)		Yes
Rel_Dt	Date		Yes
Ret_Dt	Date		
Cr	String(20)		
Pc	Number(12.2)		
Wte	String(1000)		
Image	blob		
Prop_1	String(1000)		
..			
..			
..			
Prop_50	String(1000)		

There are 50 Prop columns numbered prop_1 to prop_50

Table Name:	SKU_Prods		
Column Name	Data Type	Key	Required
SKU_No	Number(10,0)	Primary	Yes
Pd_ID	Number(10,0)	Primary	Yes

Table Name:	ORDERS		
Column Name	Data Type	Key	Required
ID	Number(20,0)	Primary	Yes
No.	Number(20,0)	Index_1 1	Yes
Od_Dt	Date	Index_2 1	Yes
Dvry_Dt	Date	Index_3 1	
Desc	String(1000)		

Table Name:	ORDITEMS		
Column Name	Data Type	Key	Required
ID	Number(20,0)	Primary	Yes
SKU_No	Number(10,0)	Index_1 2	Yes
Qty	Number(10,0)		Yes

Table Name:	CUST		
Column Name	Data Type	Key	Required
ID	Number(20,0)	Primary	Yes
No.	Number(20,0)	Index_1_1	Yes
Name	Number(10,0)	Index_1_2	Yes
Phone	String(20)	Index_2_1	Yes
Email	String(100)	Index_3_1	Yes
Address	String(100)	Index_4_1	Yes
City	String(30)	Index_5_1	Yes
State	String(30)	Index_6_1	Yes
Country	String(30)	Index_7_1	Yes
Phone_2	String(20)	Index_8_1	
Email_2	String(100)	Index_9_1	
Address_2	String(100)	Index_10_1	
City_2	String(30)	Index_11_1	
State_2	String(30)	Index_12_1	
Country_2	String(30)	Index_13_1	
Zip	String(30)		
Zip_2	String(30)		

A good database designer will recognize several problems with the tables in the supplied report. The database administrator who sent us the report is not the designer. He is the support database administrator. As usual, the designer of the above database has since been promoted and moved on after this database went into production. There has not been any opportunity to critique the database design because no one looked at it. Once the software based on the database passed user acceptance test and the users could do their work, all was assumed to be well.

Please note that a real world database will have hundreds of tables and many more columns than reported in our project. Picture hundreds of tables named as shown in the report. This is however sufficient to illustrate the poor quality.

Based on all we have learned so far, the names of the tables and columns need to be meaningful. With the current report, our first task is to clarify the table and column names with the database administrator. This first process would have been unnecessary had the designer been quality conscious. The process of clarifying the names by the support database administrator will be long because, he has to read through programs, call the original designer if possible and look at stored data to determine what the columns hold.

A good question that comes to mind is why didn't the front end developers ask for more meaningful names? The most likely reason is short sightedness. They did not foresee other potential developers that will also use this database. Once the table and column names were explained to them, they were satisfied because they had enough information to complete their tasks, probably in a hurry.

The Clarified Report From Database Administrator

Suppose we are able to get clarification three weeks later (could be months if hundreds of tables), this will add cost to our new project. The following pages contain the new report from the database administrator.

Table Name:	Prod (Products table)		
Column Name	Data Type	Key	Required
ID (Unique number generated by the database)	Number(10,0)	Primary	Yes
PN (Product Name)	String(100)	Index_1_1	Yes
Mod (Model)	String(100)	Index_1_2	Yes
Ver (Version)	String(10)	Index_1_3	Yes
Desc	String(1000)		Yes
Rel_Dt (Released date when product is first available for sale)	Date		Yes
Ret_Dt (Retired Date when product is no longer manufactured)	Date		
Cr (Product color)	String(20)		
Sz (product size, 1, 2 …)	Number(5.0)		
Wght (Weight in grams)	Number(10.4)		
Wdth (Width in centimeters)	Number(10.4)		

Lnth(Length in centimeters)	Number(10.4)		
Heht(Height in centimeters)	Number(10.4)		
Image (Picture of the product)	blob		
Manu (Manufacture of product, default is 'NotReal Corporation)	String(100)	Index_2_1	Yes
Prop_1 (Other property of the product such as speed)	String(1000)		
..			
..			
Prop_50(Other property of the product such as power)	String(1000)		

There are 50 Property columns numbered 1 to 50

Table Name:	SKUS (Product bundles table)		
Column Name	Data Type	Key	Required
SKU_No (Stock Keeping Unit number)	Number(10,0)	Prima ry	Yes
KN (Stock Keeping Unit Name)	String(100)	Index _1_1	Yes
Mod (Model)	String(100)	Index _1_2	Yes
Ver (version)	String(10)	Index _1_3	Yes
Desc (Description)	String(1000)		Yes
Rel_Dt (Release date)	Date		Yes
Ret_Dt (Retired Date)	Date		
Cr (Color)	String(20)		
Pc (Price)	Number(12.2)		
Wte (Warrantee)	String(1000)		
Image (Picture of products bundle)	blob		
Prop_1(Other property of the bundle such as power)	String(1000)		
..			
..			
Prop_50(Other property of the bundle)	String(1000)		

Table Name:	SKU_Prods (Bundle_Products)		
Column Name	Data Type	Key	Required
SKU_No (Stock Keeping Unit number)	Number(10,0)	Primary	Yes
Pd_ID (Product ID from the prod table)	Number(10,0)	Primary	Yes

Table Name:	ORDERS		
Column Name	Data Type	Key	Required
ID (Unique number generated by the database)	Number(20,0)	Primary	Yes
No. (Customer Number matching ID in CUST table	Number(20,0)	Index_1_1	Yes
Od_Dt (Order Date)	Date	Index_2_1	Yes
Dvry_Dt (Delivery Date	Date	Index_3_1	
Desc (Miscellaneous information about order)	String(1000)		

Table Name:	ORDITEMS (Contains the items for an order)		
Column Name	Data Type	Key	Required
ID (Order number matching ID in ORDERS table)	Number(20,0)	Primary	Yes
SKU_No ((Stock	Number(10,0)	Index_1_2	Yes

Keeping Unit number from SKUS table)			
Qty (Quantity of items)	Number(10,0)		Yes

Table Name:	CUST (Clients table)		
Column Name	Data Type	Key	Required
ID(Unique number generated by the database)	Number(20,0)	Primary	Yes
No. (Customer Number)	Number(20,0)	Index_1_1	Yes
Name (Client Name)	Number(10,0)	Index_1_2	Yes
Phone	String(20)	Index_2_1	Yes
Email	String(100)	Index_3_1	Yes
Address	String(100)	Index_4_1	Yes
City	String(30)	Index_5_1	Yes
State	String(30)	Index_6_1	Yes
Country	String(30)	Index_7_1	Yes
Phone_2	String(20)	Index_8_1	
Email_2	String(100)	Index_9_1	
Address_2	String(100)	Index_10_1	
City_2	String(30)	Index_11_1	
State_2	String(30)	Index_12_1	
Country_2	String(30)	Index_13_1	
Zip	String(30)		
Zip_2	String(30)		

DATABASE REDESIGN

We have learned a lot about how to create high quality software. However, as we gather information about our environment, we find that the creators of the database did not follow the standards needed for high quality. Going back to redesign a database is a major undertaking after massive amounts of software have been built on it. However, continuing to build more software on a bad database gets worse with time. The sooner the database is redesigned, the better. If business resources permit, now is the time to re-design this database. If redesign is not possible, we still have to do the best we can to create the highest quality possible.

There are hundreds of books on database design. Most of them are based on specific database software such as Oracle. These books generally take readers through all the database objects, tables, keys, stored procedures, triggers, query language and so on. What I have not seen in these books is any emphasis on the names of the database objects that a database developer creates, as it pertains to the quality of the software that will be written using the database. The discussion that will follow will not cover these database objects. Instead, we will focus on the names of the tables and columns. In addition, we will examine the long term viability of these tables and redesign the tables if necessary.

The process of designing a database varies from organization to organization. In small organizations, one software developer will be responsible for everything, database design and software development. In a large organization such as NotReal Corporation, there will be a database administration group whose function is designing and maintaining databases. In such an environment, the database designer may have little or no experience developing front end applications. Therefore, he may not be aware of the impact of his designs on the developers. During the database design phase, the software developers should consider themselves as the ultimate owners of the data and demand any improvements needed to arrive at high quality software. We will assume that NotReal Corporation has decided to redesign the database.

Whether we are responsible to redesign the database or have input for the redesign, the next few pages show what this database should be.

What Is Wrong With The Current Database?

The most obvious problems are the names of the tables and columns. Just as we have had problems understanding the structure when first presented to us, someone else will have the same problems in the future if we leave the names as is. Let's redesign the "PROD" table for illustration. What should the table be named?

Since it holds a list of our products, it should be called "PRODUCTS".
The first column "ID" contains numbers that are generated by the database system. Is "ID" a good name for this column? The answer is no. For one, there are several columns named "ID" among the tables of this database. Within a front end application, it will be difficult to determine what a database object called queryRecordSet("ID") holds without looking through several lines of code to examine the query. An appropriate name should be "PRODUCT_ID". A better name will be "PRODUCT_AUTO_GENERATED_ID". This name will be easy to understand under all circumstances. Just like "ID", the column called "PN" should be called "PRODUCT_NAME", not "NAME" so that the "NAME" in "PRODUCT" is not confused with the "NAME" in "CUST". Following these principles, the "PROD" table could be redesigned as shown below.

Table Name: PRODUCTS
Column Name
PRODUCT_AUTO_GENERATED_ID
PRODUCT_Name
PRODUCT_Model
PRODUCT_Version
PRODUCT_Description
PRODUCT_Released_date
PRODUCT_Retired_Date
Product_color
PRODUCT_Size
PRODUCT_Weight_Grams
PRODUCT_Width_Centimeters
PRODUCT_Length_Centimeters
PRODUCT_Height_Centimeters
PRODUCT_Picture
PRODUCT_Manufacturer
PRODUCT_Other_property_1
..
..
PRODUCT_Other_property_50

The new products table is self explanatory now. We probably would not have needed further clarification if the initial report from the database administrator had been as shown in this redesign. The table still has one problem. It assumes the maximum number of other properties of a product is 50, hence PRODUCT_Other_property_1 to PRODUCT_Other_property_50. This might be true today. What will happen if a new product has 52 other properties? The obvious solution is to restructure the table by adding PRODUCT_Other_property_51 and PRODUCT_Other_property_52 columns. Whenever we exceed our maximum, we will add additional columns. There are two problems with this approach: Most database software have a maximum number of columns per table. The other is some software based on this table may need to be modified every time the database is restructured.

We need a structure that can accommodate new products having more properties without restructuring our table or modifying our front end software. The next page shows the solution to this issue.

A better solution is to create three tables as follows:

Table Name:	PRODUCTS

Column Name
PRODUCT_AUTO_GENERATED_ID
PRODUCT_Name)
PRODUCT_Model
PRODUCT_Version
PRODUCT_Description
PRODUCT_Released_date
PRODUCT_Retired_Date
Product_color
PRODUCT_Size
PRODUCT_Weight_Grams
PRODUCT_Width_Centimeters
PRODUCT_Length_Centimeters
PRODUCT_Height_Centimeters
PRODUCT_Picture
PRODUCT_Manufacturer

Table Name:	PROPERTY_DEFINITIONS

Column Name
PROPERTY_DEFINITION_ID
PROPERTY_DEFINITION_Name
PROPERTY_DEFINITION_Description

Table Name:	PRODUCT_PROPERTIES
Column Name	
PRODUCT_PROPERTY_PRODUCT_ID	
PRODUCT_PROPERTY_DEFINITION_ID	
PRODUCT_PROPERTY_VALUE	

The products tables above can handle an almost unlimited number of additional properties at this point. The tables can still be made better by further normalization. Anyway, this is a good stopping point. Remember this is not a database book and we have to draw the line here before we get carried away. The most important point made here is flexibility, lack of which, has resulted in too many unnecessary updates and revisions to software.

Overall, our goal is to have clarity in our design. To that end, I hope these three tables are self explanatory. If they are not, you should try to create your own set of product tables and make them as clear as possible.

The same limitation problems exist in the "CUST" table. This table assumes that each client can have only two addresses. Furthermore, the table does not show contacts within the companies. If a sales person has ten contacts within the same company spread out in four offices, there will be ten to twenty records in the "CUST" table. In addition to contacts addresses, a typical company will have receiving address, shipping address, billing address and several others. Like the products table, the name of the "CUST" table along with its field names needs to be changed. The "CUST" table should be broken into four or more tables as follows:

"CLIENTS" will contain corporate name, unique account number and any additional corporate information such as company tax identification number.

"CLIENT_CONTACTS" will contain the names of people to contact, each with a unique identification number and the unique account number of the client.

"ADDRESSES" will contain addresses, each with a unique identification number.

"CONTACT_ADDRESSES" will match "CLIENT_CONTACTS" to "ADDRESSES".

We will not create the tables here. I suggest each reader create these tables for practice. While doing this, add information for payment, telephones, email, account representatives and all other client related information. You will probably end up with more tables.

Database Redesign Not Possible

We have seen the considerations needed to improve the database if we were given the option to redesign the database. Suppose for business reasons, we were not allowed to redesign the database, but we still want to produce very high quality software that will be easy for others to read and maintain. Our solutions will depend on the capabilities of the database software. Most database management systems have "VIEWS". A view is a database object that represents one or more tables but has no storage of its own. If the database management system supports "VIEWS" we can create a view of the products table as follows:

```
Create View PRODUCTS as
Select ID as PRODUCT_AUTO_GENERATED_ID,
PN as PRODUCT_Name,
Mod as PRODUCT_Model,
Ver as PRODUCT_Version,
Desc as PRODUCT_Description,
Rel_Dt as PRODUCT_Released_date,
Ret_Dt as PRODUCT_Retired_Date,
Cr as PRODUCT_color,
Sz as PRODUCT_Size,
Wght as PRODUCT_Weight_Grams,
Wdth as PRODUCT_Width_Centimeters,
Lnth as PRODUCT_Length_Centimeters,
Heht as PRODUCT_Height_Centimeters,
Image as PRODUCT_Picture,
Manu as PRODUCT_Manufacturer,
Prop_1 as PRODUCT_Other_property_1,
..

..
Prop_50 as PRODUCT_Other_property_50
From prod
```

The structured query language (SQL) statement above will work in several database systems. Now, instead of using "PROD", "ID" or "cr" in your program, you will use "PRODUCTS", "PRODUCT_AUTO_GENERATED_ID" and "PRODUCT_color".

The "PRODUCTS" view will be equivalent to creating the "PRODUCTS" table below:

Table Name: PRODUCTS
Column Name
PRODUCT_AUTO_GENERATED_ID
PRODUCT_Name
PRODUCT_Model
PRODUCT_Version
PRODUCT_Description
PRODUCT_Released_date
PRODUCT_Retired_Date
Product_color
PRODUCT_Size
PRODUCT_Weight_Grams
PRODUCT_Width_Centimeters
PRODUCT_Length_Centimeters
PRODUCT_Height_Centimeters
PRODUCT_Picture
PRODUCT_Manufacturer
PRODUCT_Other_property_1
..
..
PRODUCT_Other_property_50

As we have already discussed, this table has deficiencies, but the names are at least intuitive.

There are other database objects called synonyms that can be used to change non intuitive name to intuitive names. You can explore these options with your database administrator.

The "VIEW" option will allow application developers to communicate with the database administrators when problems arise since the view resides in the database. What if we were not allowed to create the "VIEW"? We can still make our code easy to ready by using "AS" clauses in our query statements.

You will use

```
Select ID as PRODUCT_AUTO_GENERATED_ID,
PN as PRODUCT_Name,
. .
. .
Prop_50 as PRODUCT_Other_property_50
From prod PRODUCTS
```

Instead of

```
Select ID,
PN,
. .
. .
Prop_50
From prod
```

Unfortunately, you can only communicate with the database administrator in terms of "PROD", "PN", and so on under this situation.

The database design section touches on areas not normally addressed or stressed in database design books. This little knowledge will make your code easier to maintain but will not make you an expert on database design. Most database books are four times the size of this book. All developers should read database design books to fully utilize the capabilities of their databases.

A lot has been said on database because it forms the bases of most software design. The clarity of the database determines the learning curve for a new maintenance staff. A well planned database can be used easily by non-information technology staff for simple data searches and reporting. As already shown, the names of database objects, such as referential integrity, are very important in understanding error messages. The same applies to indexes, database stored functions and procedures, etcetera.

Recall the error messages discussed in "Writing High Quality Code".

```
"ORA-02291: integrity constraint
(SYS_C002359) violated - parent key not
found"
```

Compared to

```
"ORA-02291: integrity constraint
(CreditCard_In_CustomerOrders_FK) violated -
parent key not found"
```

The change from SYS_C002359 to CreditCard_In_CustomerOrders_FK made a great difference in understanding the error message. Unfortunately, SYS_C002359 is more common in database designs. This happens because database developers are mostly concerned with its functionalities and rarely consider these impacts on front end software developers.

CELL PHONE SOFTWARE

In the previous discussion on database, we looked at several scenarios: whether or not we are allowed to redesign the database, and whether or not we were allowed to create "VIEWS". How will our knowledge of the database affect the design of our cell phone software?

We can make the same assumptions in the database that a client can have only two addresses and there are a maximum of fifty other properties per product. In my experience, most developers will choose this assumption and develop software that matches the current database.

We can assume that the database will be redesigned some day and develop the cell phone software to accommodate the redesign as much as possible. Given a typical work environment, pressures from managers to deliver quickly will make taking this route very difficult if not impossible. With good analysis, it might be possible to convince management that this approach will cost a lot less, when support and modifications are factored in. Remember that all software would have to be modified every time the "PROD" table has an additional column. One more consideration is the middle ware application. These same decisions must be made for the middle ware, develop as is or develop for possible future redesign.

Why Develop On A Cell Phone?

The front end of this application could easily be on a laptop computer. This would make the environment more predictable. I have chosen a cell phone just to illustrate the environmental conditions that developers take for granted when developing on a standard workstation. While these environmental conditions are more obvious on a cell phone, they exist on any computer. At the end of this section, a developer should take away the necessity to consider these variables when developing on a workstation.

We stated earlier on the definition of high quality software that software needs to be flexible enough to accommodate new business requirements without re-write or re-compile. With this in mind, let's discuss the considerations of our software for the long run.

Given: A Sophisticated Cell Phone

The sales department has already purchased the cell phone and the developers have been asked to develop based on this phone. The easiest thing to do now is get this phone, take its' configuration: storage space, operating system, screen size and resolutions, data network, etcetera, and start developing. Unfortunately, the cell phone business changes at a blinding speed. There are very many manufacturers with hundreds of models, many of which become obsolete quickly. It will be wise then to assume that the sales department will frequently purchase new types of phones that could be radically different both in operating system, size and storage capabilities.

Operating System

Today, there are several operating systems on cell phones: Linix, Windows, Black Berry, Symbian, iPhone OS, and others. Most operating systems/versions come with their software development kit (SDK) for developing applications on those particular operating systems/versions. With this, it's difficult to see how one can develop software that can run unchanged on different phones. Fortunately, there is a simple solution to this problem: J2ME, the Java 2 Micro Edition. This SDK contains a consistent platform for creating software on any operation system/version that supports this SDK. Nearly all modern cell phones support J2ME.

Data Network

A data network is needed to communicate with the middleware of our software system. There are several data network technologies and speeds used by various cell phone network carriers. The individual technologies will not be discussed here. We cannot write generic software to handle all existing and future data network technologies. Luckily, the J2ME contains data network connection classes.

Network Availability

Anyone who has used a cell phone for long will be aware of dropped calls, no service available areas, or poor signals, leading to breaking up in voice communications. The same problems that affect cell phone voice communications also affect the data networks. The connection will not always be present. Here is our first lesson on quality consideration as it relates to traditional software on a workstation. Developers always assume the network is always there and never test for its existence before trying to use it. A good wired network is present over 99 percent of the time but that is not a good reason to ignore the possibility of network failure. Ignoring the possibility of network failure could results in unpredictable software behavior. The software might hang, exit abruptly or give incomprehensive message. I have observed a call for technical support that took hours, only to find out the problem was network outage. This call could have been avoided had the software checked for network availability before trying to use it. While the software could not have prevented the outage, it could have given a clear message stating the outage and asking the users to call Network Engineering or wait for the network to be re-established before retrying their operations.

Getting back to our cell phone, how should we write this software to accommodate cell phone data networks that frequently fail as the user moves around? A synchronous communication with our middleware will be very unreliable. This calls for a background process that continually checks for data to send to the middleware and checks the middleware for data to retrieve to the cell phone. A second part of the cell phone software will handle the human interface. Thus, the user can use the software at all times and refreshes will be handled automatically when data connection is available.

Internal Storage

The storage available on cell phones is increasing but it's a tiny fraction of what is available on workstations or servers. Today, a phone with 8 gigabyte of storage is considered high while a workstation with 100 gigabyte is considered low. It is safe to assume that cell phone storage will continue to increase as new phones are developed. When our software tries to store data in our cell phone, there is no guarantee there will be enough available storage space. Any given phone has several applications using storage. Therefore, both our human interface and the background software must check for adequate storage space before trying to store data. In the event of insufficient space, the software must report an appropriate message about the insufficient storage and suggests that the user delete unnecessary data. It will also be wise to report low storage warnings when available storage drops below a certain threshold because allowing available storage to be zero could affect other applications running on the phone. Recall that high quality software must not harm other applications. If our software runs but causes others to fail, then our software is of low quality.

Here lies the second lesson for traditional programming. Developers generally do not check for storage space before writing to workstation disk. They assume that space will always be available given the size of workstation disks. Here again, I have observed a support call that took several hours to resolve when a user downloaded several movies from the internet into a workstation and caused it to run out of disk space.

Phone Screens

Cell phone screens vary considerably, both in physical size and resolution. Furthermore, some phones have landscape modes that a software must react to when the user desire landscape mode. The human interface section of our application must continuously check the screen resolution every time a screen refresh is needed. Some phones have "accelerometer sensor" or auto-rotate. This is where the screen mode changes from portrait to landscape and vice versa depending on how the user is holding the phone. Our software should react to this event. Screen resolution is yet another area that is taken for granted in traditional programming. On workstations, screen resolutions can be set by the users. Unless, a standard setting is enforced, a developer should detect screen resolution and paint the screen accordingly. I have seen software screens that look bad, too small or too large when users changed their screen resolutions. Newer cell phones with touch screens also use the screen as an input device, thereby potentially covering all or part of an application with the on-screen keyboard. Here again, this must be considered in the cell phone software for the future if possible.

Phone Input

Cell phones have several input methods; touch screens, optical mouse, handwriting recognition, Full QWERTY keyboard, numeric only keyboard, etcetera. These are the many possible combinations we must take into consideration, as opposed to a workstation with keyboard and mouse. Again, I have seen software become totally inoperable because the mouse stopped working. Developers should program for users to be able to move around and enter data with keyboard only. A simple way is to use combination keys such as "Alt L" to move to the field where the user can enter "Last Name". At a minimum, users should be able to use the "Tab" key to move in a logical manner (not randomly) through the editable fields.

MIDDLE WARE SOFTWARE

In a typical multi-tier application, the back-end is the database; the front-end is the presentation layer and the middle-tier contains the business logic. The middle-tier also has the responsibility of communication between itself and the other tiers. The main argument in support of multi-tier applications is that the front-end will not need modification should the database change (example, change from Oracle to MSSQL or the machine is moved from Dallas to Chicago). What about changes such as adding new columns? With adequate foresight, both the middle and front tiers may not need modifications. However, some changes to the database will unavoidably result in changes to both middle and front ends. This is where multi-tier applications have a maintenance disadvantage over client/server applications. In the following paragraphs, let's examine approaches to the middle-tier that could minimize re-writes.

Flexibility

We have discussed ways to create high quality software. Everything that we have learned should be applied to the middle tier. The middle tier has the special responsibility to be flexible. It should contain all current business rules and anticipate as many future changes as possible. Let's list future possible changes that we can currently anticipate.

- The number of users (currently 1500) will likely change. We need to plan for 3000 or more because NotReal Corporation is growing rapidly.

- Database structure may change (discussed under database).

- Location or type of database could change.

- Type or version of the front end cell phone could change.

- The system may need to support multiple types of cell phones simultaneously in the future.

- The front end could become laptops.

- In a real world situation, there will be many more possible changes that we can anticipate.

Configuration Files

To be able to handle anticipated changes, most requirements should be in configuration files, not hard coded. For example, the current cell phone and its capabilities should be in a configuration file. The configuration file should be structured to handle multiple phone types. When the middle tier receives a request from a phone, it should determine the type of phone and use a matching configuration to handle the request. In the beginning, there will be configuration for our current phone but adding or changing phone type should not require a re-write of the middle tier, just configuration file change.

Instead of creating a configuration file for cell phones, an alternative will be to store cell phone capabilities in the database.

Configuration files should also be created for communicating with the database, making it flexible to change or relocate the database.

Hardware Size

The hardware should be sized to handle 3000 or more users since we can easily foresee a rapid growth from the current 1500 users.

Logging

You cannot have too much log information when it comes to middle tier. The middle tier should log every transaction and exception. This is important since the middle tier typically has no screens and the only way to detect and resolve problems is by viewing the log of events.

CONSULTING SERVICES

Various software consulting services are provided by Crystal Seed, LLC.

Please visit **go2quality.com.**

To contact us please visit go2quality.com.

Code Review

Code review is the most effective way for an organization to ensure high quality of its software. Quality assurance testing is too late. By the time most software reaches quality assurance testing, thousands or even millions of code lines would have been written. If the code contains repetitions, quality assurance testing can only catch the areas that were tested, leaving wrong code un-remedied. As already stated, most quality assurance tests focus primarily on specific business requirements and very rarely test infrastructure or appropriate messages when things go wrong. Today, there are several testing methodologies, some based on frequent quality assurance testing during the development process instead of waiting till the end of development. While these methodologies help, none can take the place of code review.

The Difficulties With In-House Code Review

Code review done within a development team can be infective; hence it is often not done. Co-workers may be sensitive to each other and unwilling to point out serious flaws in each other's code.

Most reviewers do not know what to look for in reviewing another developer's code. They end up trying to ensure that business requirements are met just like quality assurance testers, the difference is reading the code instead of running the application.

Without a standard as outlined in this book, each developer will review his peer's code based on his personal standard, which may be poor.

The Case For Outside Consultants

With outside consultants who have been trained on code review, all code will be reviewed to topnotch standards of code functionalities and legibility. Error handling will be examined as well as all other factors outlined in this book. The outside consultant may not meet the developers, only phone access to ask questions. Even when the consultants are in the same vicinity as developers, the developers see code reviewer as auditors and tend to accept suggestions without ill-feelings.

Everyone Needs A Copy Of This Book

If you have completed reading this book, the first instinct is to start using all you have learned and become the sole developer that writes quality code or expert that try to educate others on quality. This will be a frustrating goal as already discussed in the book. The pressures from managers and the reward system will eventually force you to give up. To succeed in quality development and still be a hero, you should recommend to your manager that everyone read the book so that everyone is on the same page, including your manager.

Training

The information contained in this book is straight forward and most fall under common sense. Why should there be training for such simple concepts after reading the book? Formal training will re-enforce that management is serious about quality. Training will help to change the culture of haste over quality from the top down. During training, the group uses sample projects from their environment instead of the many hypothetical examples used in the book.

Software Quality Monitoring

In order to truly change the haste over quality culture, organizations must implement a system that holds development teams accountable after the deployment party. Just like code review, quality monitoring can be difficult within a group. It is best when a special team outside all development teams manage quality on an enterprise wide base. Consulting is available either as outside monitor or to help in setting up an internal monitoring team/system.